ANCHOR~~AGE~~
GUIDE 2024 -2025

Anchorage Unveiled: Your Essential Companion to Embracing the Wonders of Alaska's Gateway City

Max Sterling

1

Welcome to Anchorage

In the heart of the wild and wondrous state of Alaska lies a city that defies expectations, challenges conventions, and stirs the soul in ways unfathomable. Anchorage—a name that conjures images of untamed landscapes, majestic wildlife, and a harmony of cultures—is more than a destination; it's an odyssey into the heart of human curiosity and nature's grandeur.

Imagine a city where the aurora dances across the night sky, where glaciers stand as silent sentinels, and where the vibrant energy of a cosmopolitan center melds seamlessly with the tranquility of pristine wilderness. Anchorage is a tapestry of contradictions woven together with an unmistakable Alaskan spirit—a spirit that embraces the rugged and the refined, the familiar and the extraordinary.

In this enchanting realm, where mountains and fjords meet urban streets, Anchorage captivates with its raw beauty and diverse narratives. It's a place where dreams of scaling summits and witnessing the Northern Lights intertwine with aspirations of culinary exploration and cultural immersion. Anchorage is where the heart races with anticipation and the soul finds solace in nature's embrace.

As you journey through these pages, prepare to be immersed in tales of discovery, where each corner turned reveals a new facet of Anchorage's identity. From the bustling streets of downtown to the serene trails of the Chugach Mountains, every chapter unveils the layers of a city that nurtures the adventurous spirit, invites the open-hearted traveler, and leaves an indelible mark on those fortunate enough to explore its landscapes and stories.

Join us as we traverse Anchorage's urban heartbeats, traverse its untamed wilderness, and connect with its welcoming community. Anchorage is not just a place to visit; it's an experience that ignites the senses, captivates the imagination, and etches lasting memories in the depths of your heart. Welcome to Anchorage—where dreams are realized, and the untamed soul of Alaska becomes your own.

Anchorage Essentials

Weather and When to Go

Nestled within the picturesque landscapes of Alaska, Anchorage stands as a vibrant metropolis that bridges the gap between untamed wilderness and modern urbanity. This duality is the cornerstone of its allure, where the imposing Chugach Mountains harmoniously coexist with a dynamic downtown culture. Anchorage's profound connection to its indigenous heritage is palpable, displayed through captivating art, traditional festivals, and intriguing museums that provide insight into both historical and contemporary Alaskan lifestyles.

Embarking on a Seasonal Journey:

Winter (December to February): Anchorage dons a blanket of snow, captivating the city in a tranquil hush during these months. Embrace the bracing chill as you immerse yourself in a realm of winter sports and exhilarating activities. Skiing and snowboarding enthusiasts find their haven on the local slopes, while ice skating rinks and frozen lakes invite you to glide amid the wintry magic. The world-renowned Iditarod sled dog race, an emblem of Alaskan spirit, adds an exhilarating touch to winter. However, be mindful of the limited daylight hours, which can influence your exploration plans.

Spring (March to May): Anchorage undergoes a gradual transformation as the temperatures rise and the snow begins to yield to the warmth of the sun. Witness nature's reawakening as wildlife emerges from their winter havens and flowers start to bloom, painting the city in vibrant hues. Photographers find inspiration in the transition from the crisp whiteness of winter to the vibrant colors of spring, capturing moments of transformation unique to this time of year.

Summer (June to August): Anchorage's summer is a symphony of activity and sunlight. The city experiences its peak tourist season during these months, a period defined by long daylight hours often referred to as the "midnight sun." The warm embrace of the sun opens doors to a myriad of outdoor pursuits. Wander along the Tony Knowles Coastal Trail to observe beluga whales playing in the inlet, or venture further into the pristine wilderness of Chugach State Park. The Anchorage Market and Festival, an open-air bazaar of culture and creativity, embodies the heart of the city's lively spirit.

Fall (September to November): Fall arrives with a gentle chill in the air and a stunning transformation of foliage. The landscape morphs into a canvas of red and gold hues, painting a vivid tapestry that is perfect for hikers and photographers alike. September's enchanting ambiance extends to the waters as salmon make their final journey upstream, making it an opportune time for fishing enthusiasts. As the season progresses, however, some amenities and attractions might close in preparation for the impending winter.

Crafting the Perfect Visit:

Summer (June to August): The summer season is undoubtedly the most popular among tourists. The warm weather and extended daylight hours ensure a plethora of outdoor activities, cultural experiences, and exploration opportunities. Just be ready for higher costs and bustling crowds.

Late Spring (May) and Early Fall (September): These transition periods offer a wonderful compromise between favorable weather and fewer tourists. The city's ambiance is more relaxed, accommodations might be more affordable, and you can enjoy the beauty of Anchorage with a touch of serenity.

Winter (December to February): If you crave an adventure amid a snowy wonderland or wish to witness the Iditarod, the winter months are tailor-made for you. However, brace yourself for cold temperatures and the shorter days that characterize this season.

Navigating Anchorage's Dynamic Weather:

Anchorage's climate is as diverse as its landscapes, and rapid weather shifts are a characteristic feature.

Pack smartly with layers, waterproof clothing, and durable footwear to embrace whatever Mother Nature presents. An adaptable wardrobe will ensure you're always comfortable, regardless of the atmospheric whims.

In closing, Anchorage is an all-season treasure trove, each period offering a distinct chapter of its allure. The interplay between nature's grandeur and the city's cultural richness paints a remarkable canvas for explorers. By aligning your visit with the seasons that resonate with your interests, you'll embark on a journey that uncovers Anchorage's multifaceted charm in all its glory.

Practical Tips for Travelers

Dress in Layers:

Anchorage's climate is characterized by its variability, so dressing in layers is a smart strategy. Start with a moisture-wicking base layer, add insulating layers like fleece or down, and finish with waterproof and windproof outerwear. This flexibility allows you to adjust to the changing temperatures and conditions as you explore the city.

Waterproof Footwear:

Anchorage's weather can include rain, snow, and slush, especially during the shoulder seasons. Having waterproof footwear, such as insulated boots or waterproof hiking shoes, will keep your feet warm and dry as you navigate wet sidewalks, snowy trails, and potentially muddy paths.

Sun Protection:

In the summer months, Anchorage experiences the "midnight sun," with extended daylight hours. Protect yourself from the sun's rays by wearing sunglasses with UV protection, a wide-brimmed hat to shade your face and neck, and applying sunscreen to exposed skin. Even on overcast days, UV rays can still be strong.

Insect Repellent:

Alaska's lush landscapes can bring out mosquitoes and other biting insects during certain times of the year. Carry an effective insect repellent to prevent discomfort and potential bites while enjoying outdoor activities.

Carry a Water Bottle:

Stay hydrated, especially during active pursuits. A reusable water bottle is a practical essential. Many public spaces in Anchorage offer water refill stations, making it easy to stay refreshed throughout your day.

Wildlife Safety:

Venturing into Anchorage's wilder areas comes with the potential for wildlife encounters. Research how to respond to encounters with animals like moose and bears, and carry bear spray as a precaution if you're exploring beyond the city limits.

Research Aurora Borealis Viewing:

For those seeking the awe-inspiring Northern Lights during the winter, research prime viewing locations away from city lights, monitor aurora forecasts, and consider booking a tour with experienced guides who can lead you to the best vantage points.

Currency and Payments:

Credit cards are widely accepted, but it's advisable to carry some cash for small businesses, markets, or situations where cards might not be accepted. Notify your bank about your travel plans to avoid any unexpected card issues.

Public Transportation and Parking:

Public transportation in Anchorage is convenient and eco-friendly, providing easy access to major attractions and downtown. If you opt for a rental car, be prepared for potential challenges in finding parking, especially during busy times.

Local Cuisine:

Indulge in Anchorage's culinary delights, particularly its fresh seafood offerings. Don't miss the chance to savor Alaskan king crab, salmon, and halibut. Explore local markets and eateries to immerse yourself in the region's gastronomic scene.

Emergency Contact Information:

Always carry emergency contact information, including local emergency services, your country's embassy or consulate, and the contact information of your accommodation. Being prepared for unexpected situations is paramount.

Plan for Mobile Connectivity:

While Anchorage has good mobile coverage in urban areas, remote locations might have limited or no reception. Download offline maps and apps to ensure you can navigate even in areas with poor connectivity.

Respect the Environment:

Alaska's natural beauty is its treasure, and responsible travel is essential. Adhere to Leave No Trace principles, follow park regulations, and respect wildlife from a safe distance. Contribute to the preservation of Anchorage's pristine landscapes.

Time Zone Awareness:

Anchorage operates on the Alaska Time Zone (AKT), which might differ from your home time zone. Adjust your schedule accordingly to make the most of your time and appointments.

Check Opening Hours:

To avoid disappointments verify the opening hours of attractions, restaurants, and businesses. Check online or call ahead before venturing out.

With these practical tips at your disposal, your journey to Anchorage will be well-prepared and smooth, allowing you to fully immerse yourself in the city's unique fusion of natural wonders and urban experiences. Anchorage's beauty, charm, and adventure await, ready to be explored and enjoyed to the fullest.

Safety and Health Considerations

Anchorage, with its blend of natural splendor and urban experiences, is a destination that promises captivating adventures. To ensure your journey is both enjoyable and secure, it's crucial to be informed about safety and health considerations that are unique to this Alaskan city.

Wildlife Awareness:

Alaska's wild landscapes mean that encounters with wildlife are possible, even within the city limits. Moose, in particular, are a common sight. While they may seem docile, they can become aggressive if they feel threatened. Keep a safe distance, especially during calving season. If venturing into wilderness areas, carry bear spray, learn how to use it, and be aware of local guidelines for wildlife encounters.

Outdoor Safety:

Whether you're hiking, biking, or exploring trails, make sure to share your plans with someone you trust and carry essentials like emergency supplies. Weather conditions can change quickly, so dress appropriately, pack layers, and stay hydrated. It's advisable to avoid solo adventures in remote areas, especially if you're not experienced in navigating the wilderness.

Weather Preparedness:

Anchorage's weather can be challenging due to its variability. Keep an eye on weather forecasts before heading out and be prepared for sudden changes. Dress in layers, carry waterproof gear, and be cautious of icy sidewalks and trails in colder months.

Health Considerations:

Alaska is known for its pristine environment, but it's still wise to take precautions. Drink clean and treated water to avoid waterborne illnesses. If you're planning outdoor activities, consider insect repellent to protect against mosquitoes and ticks. While medical facilities are available in Anchorage, it's always recommended to have travel insurance that covers medical emergencies.

Road Safety:

If you're driving, particularly in winter, familiarize yourself with driving conditions and safety guidelines. Snow and ice can make roads slippery, so drive cautiously and adhere to local speed limits. If you're not used to driving in such conditions, consider using public transportation instead.

Avalanche Safety:

For winter sports enthusiasts, the allure of the backcountry might be strong. However, avalanches pose a significant risk. If you're planning to venture into avalanche-prone areas, educate yourself about avalanche safety, carry proper equipment, and consider going with a knowledgeable guide.

Emergency Services:

Save local emergency numbers in your phone, including those of medical services, the police, and your country's embassy or consulate. Having these numbers on hand can provide peace of mind in case of unexpected situations.

Personal Belongings:

While Anchorage is generally safe, take basic precautions to safeguard your belongings. Use hotel safes when available, be mindful of your surroundings, and avoid displaying valuable items in public.

Local Customs and Culture:

Respect the local customs and culture, including indigenous traditions. Educate yourself about appropriate behavior, especially when participating in cultural events or visiting sacred sites.

Altitude Considerations:

Certain outdoor activities might take you to higher altitudes, which can affect some individuals, particularly those who are not accustomed to it. Stay hydrated, take breaks, and listen to your body.

By understanding and embracing these safety and health considerations, you'll be better equipped to fully enjoy your time in Anchorage. Balancing adventure with caution allows you to create unforgettable memories in this captivating city while prioritizing your well-being.

The Anchorage Survival Guide

Transportation Tips and Tricks

Public Transportation - People Mover Bus Network:

Anchorage's People Mover bus system is a reliable and eco-friendly way to traverse the city. With routes covering key areas like downtown, Midtown, and South Anchorage, you can easily reach major attractions and neighborhoods. To maximize convenience, check routes and schedules ahead of time, and consider purchasing a day pass if you anticipate multiple bus rides in a single day.

Bike Rentals and Trails - Pedaling Through Anchorage:

Immerse yourself in Anchorage's bike-friendly culture by renting a bicycle. The city boasts a well-connected network of bike lanes and trails, including the famous Tony Knowles Coastal Trail. This picturesque trail treats cyclists to panoramic vistas of the coastline and majestic mountains. Many bike rental shops provide maps and equipment, ensuring a comfortable and scenic ride.

Car Rentals - Unlocking Flexibility:

For those keen on exploring Anchorage's outskirts and beyond, renting a car offers flexibility and convenience. Keep in mind that parking in downtown Anchorage can be a challenge, particularly during peak hours. To avoid parking hassles, plan ahead by researching available parking options or using designated parking structures.

Ride-Sharing and Taxis - Door-to-Door Convenience:

Ride-sharing services and taxis offer door-to-door transportation for those seeking direct routes or destinations not easily accessible by public transportation. This option is especially beneficial if you're looking for convenient travel within the city.

Anchorage Trolley Tours - City Narratives in Motion:

Enhance your understanding of Anchorage's history, culture, and landmarks by embarking on an Anchorage trolley tour. These engaging tours provide narrated guides and often offer hop-on-hop-off options. This approach allows you to explore attractions at your own pace while soaking in the city's stories.

Airport Shuttles - Seamless Transfers:

Many Anchorage hotels provide airport shuttle services, streamlining your journey to and from the airport. When arranging your accommodations, inquire about shuttle availability to ensure smooth airport transfers.

Anchorage Railroads - Scenic Train Adventures:

For a one-of-a-kind experience, discover Anchorage's surroundings through the lens of scenic train rides. The Alaska Railroad offers journeys that showcase the state's diverse landscapes, from lush forests to grandiose mountains. Immerse yourself in the breathtaking views that unfold outside your window.

Walking the Downtown Core - Strolling Through Urban Charm:

Anchorage's compact downtown core beckons pedestrians with its pedestrian-friendly layout. Roam through the city center's streets, where you'll discover an array of shops, restaurants, galleries, and cultural attractions. Exploring on foot allows you to fully absorb the urban ambiance.

Plan for Seasonal Changes - Adapting to the Elements:

Anchorage's transportation options can be influenced by seasonal shifts. During winter, road conditions and the availability of outdoor transportation activities may differ from the summer months. Stay informed and adapt your plans accordingly.

Be Prepared for Remote Areas - Navigating the Unplugged Zones:

If your exploration takes you to remote or wilderness areas surrounding Anchorage, be aware that cell reception might be limited or absent. Prioritize offline maps or navigation tools to navigate these situations effectively.

Use Anchorage's Free Downtown Shuttle - Seamless Urban Exploration:

During the summer months, take advantage of the complimentary Anchorage Downtown Partnership Shuttle. This convenient service loops around downtown, offering hop-on-hop-off opportunities to explore various attractions without worrying about parking or directions.

Consider Local Tours - Guided Adventures with Transport Included:

Anchorage boasts an array of guided tours, ranging from wildlife encounters to glacier hikes. These tours often include transportation, eliminating logistical concerns and allowing you to fully immerse yourself in Alaska's captivating scenery and unique experiences.

Check for Special Events - Navigating Event Impact:

Throughout the year, Anchorage hosts diverse events and festivals that can influence traffic and parking availability. Stay updated by consulting local event calendars to ensure your transportation plans align smoothly with these occasions.

Park-and-Ride Facilities - Effortless Urban Exploration:

When driving into the city, consider utilizing park-and-ride facilities located on the outskirts of downtown. These facilities enable you to park your vehicle and seamlessly transition to public transportation for hassle-free exploration of the city center.

Embrace Alaskan Ferries - Coastal Adventures Afloat:

If your travel aspirations encompass nearby islands or coastal areas, indulging in an Alaskan ferry experience offers a distinctive viewpoint to appreciate the captivating coastal landscapes. Enjoy the allure of the sea as you explore the Alaskan shoreline from a unique vantage point.

Traversing Anchorage is an adventure in itself, with a plethora of transportation options to suit your preferences. Whether you're navigating city streets, embarking on guided tours, or venturing into the wilderness, these transportation tips and tricks are designed to enhance your Anchorage experience, ensuring seamless exploration of its captivating landscapes and vibrant culture.

Currency, Banking, and Budgeting

Currency:

The US Dollar (USD) reigns as the official currency not only in Anchorage but also across the United States. With banknotes ranging from the humble $1 bill to the more substantial $100 bill, and a collection of coins including the penny (1¢), nickel (5¢), dime (10¢), quarter (25¢), and dollar ($1 coin, less commonly used), your financial transactions will be seamlessly conducted in these familiar denominations.

Banking Services:

Anchorage boasts a robust banking infrastructure, accommodating both local residents and visitors. A diverse array of banks, credit unions, and ATMs cater to your financial needs. Nationally recognized institutions such as Wells Fargo, Bank of America, and U.S. Bank have a strong presence in the city, offering a plethora of services. From basic transactions to currency exchange, checking and savings accounts, and even loan provisions, these institutions form a cornerstone of the city's financial landscape.

ATMs and Cash Withdrawals:

Accessing cash is a breeze in Anchorage, thanks to the widespread availability of ATMs. Conveniently situated in prime locations like shopping districts, hotels, airports, and tourist hubs, these ATMs support major credit and debit cards. It's important to be mindful of potential additional fees when using ATMs not affiliated with your bank.

Credit Cards:

Embrace the convenience of credit cards, which are widely accepted in Anchorage. Your Visa, MasterCard, American Express, and Discover cards will smoothly facilitate transactions for dining, shopping, accommodation booking, and more. To ensure seamless card usage, alert your bank about your travel dates and destination, helping you avoid security-related inconveniences.

Budgeting Tips:

- **Accommodation:** Accommodation costs span a spectrum, contingent on the type and location. Downtown lodgings or hotels near attractions may command higher rates, whereas budget-conscious travelers can consider options like hostels or cozy bed and breakfast spots.
- **Dining:** Anchorage's culinary landscape accommodates various budgets. While high-end dining establishments offer exquisite experiences, an abundance of budget-friendly choices, including food trucks, local diners, and cafes, cater to diverse palates. For frugal foodies, grocery stores provide a savvy option for self-prepared meals.

- **Transportation:** Public transportation, exemplified by buses and trolleys, offers cost-effective mobility. When renting a car, engage in comparison shopping to secure the most favorable rates. Keep tabs on fuel prices, which can oscillate.
- **Activities and Attractions:** Anchorage's outdoor gems often come with minimal entry fees or are entirely free. Allocate funds for special experiences, guided tours, and museum visits to enrich your itinerary.
- **Shopping:** Anchorage's shopping realm spans the spectrum from upscale boutiques to local craft markets. Budget appropriately to procure souvenirs, clothing, and distinctive Alaskan treasures.
- **Outdoor Adventures:** If outdoor escapades like wildlife tours, glacier hikes, or fishing expeditions beckon, research and allocate resources for these anticipated experiences.
- **Tipping:** Tipping is customary in the United States and is an integral part of the service industry. Be prepared to tip 15-20% of the total bill at restaurants, and extend gratuities to hotel staff, tour guides, and taxi drivers as well.

Currency Exchange:

While currency exchange services can often be found at major airports and certain banks, it's recommended to exchange currency before embarking on your journey or upon arrival in Anchorage if necessary. The prevalence of credit cards and ATMs has streamlined financial transactions, making it sufficient to carry a small amount of local currency for daily expenses.

Emergency Contacts:

In the event of financial hiccups, having your bank's customer service or hotline contact information is invaluable. Additionally, safeguard your card numbers and crucial contact details in a secure location separate from your physical cards.

Crafting Your Budget and Embracing the Adventure:

Tailoring your budget to your preferences and planned activities is pivotal for a rewarding Anchorage adventure. With meticulous planning and an understanding of local banking and currency nuances, your financial journey will be seamless. This leaves you unburdened to revel in the city's arresting natural beauty and cultural treasures, ensuring an Anchorage escapade to cherish.

Staying Connected: Wi-Fi and Communication
Wi-Fi Availability:

Anchorage, as a modern city, offers widespread Wi-Fi coverage in various public places such as cafes, restaurants, hotels, and even some outdoor spaces.

Many accommodations, from budget to upscale, provide complimentary Wi-Fi for guests, allowing you to stay connected during your stay.

Cellular Coverage:

Cellular coverage in Anchorage is generally reliable and widespread, particularly in urban areas. Major carriers like AT&T, Verizon, T-Mobile, and Sprint offer good coverage throughout the city. However, keep in mind that if you venture into remote wilderness areas around Anchorage, you might experience reduced or no signal reception.

International Roaming:

If you're an international traveler, check with your mobile provider about international roaming options. Some plans include data and calling packages that can be activated before your trip, allowing you to use your phone without incurring high roaming charges.

Prepaid SIM Cards:

For travelers staying in Anchorage for an extended period or wanting a local phone number, consider purchasing a prepaid SIM card from one of the major carriers. This can provide you with cost-effective local calling, texting, and data options.

Free Public Wi-Fi Spots:

Downtown Anchorage offers free public Wi-Fi in several areas, including parks, plazas, and the Anchorage Museum. Check local maps or city websites for designated Wi-Fi zones, where you can connect to the internet without using your cellular data.

Internet Cafes and Libraries:

If you need a dedicated space to work or browse the internet, you can find internet cafes and public libraries around Anchorage that offer computers with internet access. These can be useful if you don't have your own device with you.

Messaging Apps:

Using messaging apps like WhatsApp, Telegram, or Facebook Messenger can be a cost-effective way to communicate with friends and family back home, especially if you have access to Wi-Fi. These apps allow you to send texts, make calls, and even share media without incurring international SMS or calling charges.

Video Calls:

For face-to-face conversations with loved ones, video-calling services like Skype, Zoom, and FaceTime can be valuable tools. Just ensure you're connected to a stable Wi-Fi network to ensure smooth communication.

Offline Maps and Apps:

To navigate Anchorage and its surroundings without relying on data, download offline maps and navigation apps before you travel. This way, you can explore without worrying about connectivity issues.

Communication Tips:

Keep in mind that Anchorage's time zone might differ from your home country's, so factor in time differences when making calls. Also, if you're in a remote area, save your important contacts offline in case you lose signal.

Local Calling Codes:

Anchorage's area code is 907. If you're making local calls, remember to include the area code before the phone number. For international calls, use the appropriate country code.

Emergency Services:

Familiarize yourself with local emergency numbers, including those for police, medical assistance, and fire services. Keep these numbers saved in your phone in case of any unforeseen situations.

In Anchorage, staying connected is relatively straightforward, with a range of options for both Wi-Fi and cellular communication. Whether you're enjoying the city's amenities or venturing into its natural wonders, these communication strategies will help you make the most of your time while staying in touch with those who matter most.

Local Etiquette and Cultural Insights

Respect for Indigenous Cultures:

Anchorage is located in an area with a rich indigenous heritage. Show respect for Alaska Native cultures by learning about their traditions, history, and art. If attending cultural events or visiting museums, be open to understanding the significance behind their practices.

Greeting with a Smile:

Alaskans are known for their warm and friendly nature. When meeting locals, a smile and a friendly greeting go a long way in creating positive interactions. Handshakes are a common form of greeting, and a firm but not overpowering handshake is appreciated.

Being Punctual:

Punctuality is valued in Anchorage. Whether it's a business meeting, a tour, or a social gathering, arriving on time shows respect for others' schedules. If you're running late, a simple phone call to let them know is courteous.

Giving Space:

Alaskans often value their personal space. While they are friendly, it's important to respect people's physical boundaries. Maintain a comfortable distance during conversations and interactions, especially with individuals you're meeting for the first time.

Tipping and Service Industry:

Tipping is customary in Anchorage and throughout the United States. In restaurants, it's customary to leave a gratuity of around 15-20% of the bill for good service. Tipping hotel staff, tour guides, and other service providers is also appreciated.

Engaging in Conversations:

Alaskans are open to conversations and interactions, but it's considered polite to start with a friendly greeting or small talk before delving into more serious topics. Avoid jumping directly into business matters or personal questions without establishing a rapport.

By understanding and respecting these local etiquette and cultural insights, you'll not only enhance your own travel experience but also contribute positively to the community you're visiting. Anchorage's cultural tapestry is a wonderful aspect of the city's allure, and embracing it will undoubtedly enrich your journey.

Emergency Contacts and Services

Emergency Services: 911

In case of immediate danger, medical emergencies, or accidents, dial 911 for prompt assistance. The emergency dispatch center will connect you with police, fire, or medical services as needed.

Anchorage Police Department:

Non-emergency inquiries and assistance can be directed to the Anchorage Police Department. They can provide information, report incidents, and offer assistance for various non-life-threatening situations.

- **Non-Emergency Line: 907-786-8900**

Medical Services:

For medical emergencies and healthcare needs, Anchorage has a range of medical facilities offering top-quality care.

- **Providence Alaska Medical Center**: Anchorage's largest hospital providing a full spectrum of medical services.
- Address: 3200 Providence Drive, Anchorage
- Contact: 907-562-2211

Alaska Regional Hospital: Another major healthcare facility catering to various medical needs.

- Address: 2801 DeBarr Road, Anchorage
- Contact: 907-276-1131

Poison Control Center:

In case of accidental poisoning or exposure to toxic substances, you can reach out to the Alaska Poison Control Center for guidance.

- **Toll-Free Number:** 1-800-222-1222

Fire Department:

For fire-related emergencies or to report fires, contact the Anchorage Fire Department.

- **Non-Emergency Line: 907-267-4900**

Roadside Assistance:

If you encounter vehicle breakdowns or issues on the road, several roadside assistance services operate in Anchorage.

- **AAA Alaska:** Offers roadside assistance, travel planning, and more.
- **Toll-Free Number:** 1-800-AAA-HELP

Embassy and Consulate Information:

If you're a foreign traveler and require assistance from your home country's diplomatic representatives, here is the information for some embassies/consulates in Anchorage:

Canadian Consulate: For Canadian citizens

- **Address:** 3601 C Street, Suite 1300, Anchorage
- **Contact:** 907-271-5966

Russian Consulate: For Russian citizens

- **Address:** 3581 Denali Street, Suite 202, Anchorage
- **Contact:** 907-272-1481

Mental Health Support:

If you or someone you know is in need of mental health support, there are resources available to provide assistance.

- **Alaska Careline:** Offers emotional support and crisis intervention.
- **Toll-Free Helpline:** 1-877-266-4357 (HELP)

Lost or Stolen Items:

If you lose something valuable or experience theft during your visit, it's recommended to contact the local police and file a report. This can be useful for insurance claims and potential recovery efforts.

Severe Weather Alerts:

For information about severe weather alerts and emergency notifications, you can tune in to local news channels, radio stations, and follow official social media accounts of relevant authorities.

Safe Travels:

Prior to your trip, share your itinerary and contact details with a trusted friend or family member, and keep a copy of important contacts and documents in a secure location.

Language Assistance:

While English is widely spoken, having access to translation services or language apps can be helpful in case of communication challenges.

In times of emergency or uncertainty, it's essential to remain calm and seek assistance from the appropriate resources. Anchorage's emergency services and support systems are designed to ensure the safety and well-being of residents and visitors alike. Familiarize yourself with these contacts to have a comprehensive safety net as you explore the captivating city of Anchorage.

Understanding Anchorage's History

Tracing the Native Heritage

Anchorage's Indigenous Legacy:

Nestled within the heart of Alaska, Anchorage is not only a modern city but also a gateway to the rich tapestry of Alaska's indigenous cultures. The city stands on the ancestral lands of the Dena'ina Athabascan people, whose heritage is interwoven with the very fabric of the region. Anchorage pays homage to its native roots through museums, cultural centers, and events that provide a captivating glimpse into the traditions, history, and vibrant lives of Alaska's original inhabitants.

Dena'ina Athabascan People:

The Dena'ina Athabascan people have called the Anchorage area home for thousands of years. Their close connection to the land, waterways, and wildlife has shaped their cultural practices, art, and spiritual beliefs. Their legacy endures in modern Anchorage, where efforts to honor and preserve their traditions are evident in various aspects of the city's identity.

Anchorage Museum's Native Collections:

The Anchorage Museum serves as a bridge between the past and the present, offering a profound insight into Alaska's native cultures. Its comprehensive collection of artifacts, art, and cultural exhibits showcases the ingenuity, artistic expression, and lifestyles of the native communities. Visitors can explore intricate beadwork, traditional tools, ceremonial regalia, and contemporary art that pay homage to the Dena'ina and other indigenous groups.

Alaska Native Heritage Center:

For an immersive experience in Anchorage's native heritage, the Alaska Native Heritage Center is a must-visit. This cultural institution offers interactive exhibits, demonstrations, and performances that shed light on the Dena'ina Athabascan people as well as other indigenous groups from across Alaska. Stroll through recreated traditional dwellings, watch traditional dances, and engage with native artisans as they demonstrate their craftsmanship.

Festivals and Celebrations:

Anchorage comes alive with native heritage during various events and festivals. The "Fur Rendezvous" or "Fur Rondy," an annual winter festival, features native arts and crafts, cultural displays, and traditional games. Additionally, the "We Are All Related" gathering celebrates the connections between indigenous communities and offers a platform for sharing stories and traditions.

Preserving Traditions:

Efforts to honor native heritage extend beyond museums and events. Anchorage's street names, art installations, and public spaces often bear native names, showcasing the commitment to preserving the essence of the Dena'ina Athabascan culture. Many businesses, guided tours, and cultural programs are led by native Alaskans, offering travelers an opportunity to learn directly from those who carry forward these ancient traditions.

Connecting with the Community:

To truly immerse yourself in Anchorage's native heritage, consider participating in guided tours and workshops led by native community members. Learn traditional crafting techniques, discover the significance of storytelling, and gain insights into the harmonious relationship between indigenous people and their environment.

Respectful Engagement:

When engaging with native heritage, it's crucial to approach it with respect and an open heart. Indigenous cultures hold deep spiritual and cultural significance, and taking the time to learn, listen, and appreciate their stories fosters a meaningful connection with both the past and present.

In Conclusion:

Tracing the native heritage in Anchorage is a profound journey that unveils the Dena'ina Athabascan people's enduring legacy. Anchorage's commitment to preserving, celebrating, and sharing indigenous traditions offers travelers a unique opportunity to connect with the ancient soul of Alaska, fostering an understanding of its vibrant past and its integral role in the city's present identity.

Gold Rush Days and Early Settlement

In the heart of Alaska's history lies the captivating chapter of Gold Rush days that shaped Anchorage's early settlement. This era, synonymous with the allure of riches and the pursuit of dreams, left an indelible mark on the city's identity. Anchorage's origins are tightly interwoven with the tales of prospectors, adventurers, and pioneers who flocked to the region in pursuit of the golden promise hidden within its rugged landscapes.

The Spark of the Gold Rush:

The late 1800s witnessed a phenomenon that would forever etch its mark on Alaska's landscape: the Gold Rush. This captivating era was characterized by the allure of wealth, drawing individuals from across the globe to the untouched wilderness of the North. Anchorage, positioned between the rugged Chugach Mountains and the sweeping shores of Cook Inlet, became a focal point during this feverish time. While not the epicenter, its strategic location made it a bustling waypoint for those en route to distant goldfields, a transient hub buzzing with dreams and aspirations.

Tent City and the Railroad:

As the 20th century dawned, the area that would become Anchorage transformed into a "Tent City," a dynamic settlement pulsating with life. The canvas of the landscape was painted with tents and makeshift structures that housed a motley crew of miners, traders, and visionaries. Amid this makeshift town, a transformative force was on the horizon—the Alaska Railroad. Completed in 1923, this steel artery not only connected Anchorage to remote parts of the state but also solidified the city's role in Alaska's development. Anchorage's future was no longer merely linked to gold; it was intertwined with the broader aspirations of a burgeoning region.

Matanuska Colony: A Tale of Resilience:

The 1930s cast a shadow of economic turmoil across the globe, and Anchorage's history was once again marked by transformation. In the depths of the Great Depression, President Franklin D. Roosevelt's New Deal gave rise to the Matanuska Colony, an endeavor that saw families from the Midwest transplanted to the fertile Matanuska Valley. Anchorage became the gateway to this new chapter, symbolizing not only the resilience of those who sought opportunity but also the city's evolving identity as a haven of possibilities.

Preserving Anchorage's History: Gold Rush Days:

While Anchorage has evolved into a modern metropolis, its historical tapestry is carefully preserved through events like Gold Rush Days. This annual celebration is a time machine to eras gone by, a vivid journey back to the days of pioneers and prospectors. With period costumes, parades, and reenactments, visitors are transported to a time when dreams of striking it rich and shaping a future were the driving forces.

Exploring the Echoes of History:

Anchorage today is a vibrant blend of past and present, and visitors have a plethora of avenues to explore its rich legacy:

Alaska Native Heritage Center: While not directly tied to the Gold Rush, this center is a portal to Alaska's indigenous cultures, offering insight into the roots that predate the era of prospectors.

Anchorage Museum: This institution serves as a portal to Anchorage's evolution, with exhibits tracing the city's journey from the Gold Rush era to its contemporary identity.

Delaney Park Strip: Originally the home of Tent City, this park now stands as a tranquil space, a tangible link to Anchorage's beginnings.

Anchorage's Timeless Tapestry:

Anchorage's Gold Rush Days and its early settlement era are the foundation stones of the city's identity. The stories of those who dared to dream of fortune, the tenacity of pioneers, and the cultural threads woven into the city's fabric create a tapestry of historical significance. Amid the backdrop of modernity, the echoes of the past resonate in traditions, events, and landmarks, inviting visitors to step into a bygone era while embracing the present. Anchorage's history is not just a chronicle; it's a vibrant living entity that enriches the experiences of all who walk its streets.

Anchorage's Role in World War II

Nestled within the breathtaking landscapes of Alaska, Anchorage unveils a lesser-known facet of its history—a chapter where its natural beauty intersected with the strategic necessities of World War II. This vital port city, celebrated for its diverse culture and scenic wonders, emerged as a pivotal military hub that significantly influenced the course of the war.

Strategic Importance: Anchorage's Commanding Position:

As the United States faced the challenges of World War II, Anchorage's geographical location became a beacon of strategic importance. Situated on the fringes of the Pacific Ocean, the city became a gateway to multiple critical fronts. Anchorage served as a vital link connecting the U.S. mainland with the Aleutian Islands and the Russian Far East. Its proximity was invaluable for both defensive preparations and offensive initiatives, as the U.S. military sought to guard American soil and counter potential threats.

Alaskan Highway and Military Fortifications:

Amidst this critical backdrop, the construction of the Alaska Highway—also known as the Alcan Highway—emerged as a monumental achievement. Spanning over 1,500 miles of challenging terrain and wilderness, this highway became the lifeline that connected Anchorage to the contiguous United States. Its creation facilitated the swift movement of troops, supplies, and equipment, elevating the efficiency of the defense strategy.

Anchorage transformed into a home for various military installations, each playing a distinctive role in the war effort. Elmendorf Field, a site that has evolved into the present-day Joint Base Elmendorf-Richardson, rose as a significant air base. It served as a vital hub for aircraft refueling and maintenance, supporting transcontinental flights to and from the Asian theater. Meanwhile, Fort Richardson, initially designed to safeguard the territory from possible invasion, evolved into an indispensable training and logistical nucleus.

The Aleutian Campaign: A Display of Resilience:

Anchorage's influence extended beyond its borders to the remote Aleutian Islands—a theater often overshadowed by other fronts. The Aleutian Campaign aimed to thwart Japan's attempts to establish footholds in the Pacific. Anchorage's U.S. military forces launched operations to recapture occupied islands and secure the region, highlighting both the city's projection of American power and its resilience in a challenging environment.

Economic and Social Transformations: Anchorage's Ongoing Evolution:

World War II ushered in transformative changes for Anchorage. The influx of military personnel and extensive construction projects injected fresh energy into the local economy, propelling growth and development. The city's social fabric was enriched by the presence of soldiers and civilians from diverse backgrounds, leading to a lasting impact on its identity.

Legacy and Remembrance: Anchorage's Enduring Tribute:

In the present day, Anchorage's World War II legacy lives on through a tapestry of historical sites, museums, and memorials. The Alaska Veterans Museum stands as a poignant tribute to those who served, honoring their sacrifices and contributions. The Anchorage War Memorial serves as a solemn reminder of the trials and sacrifices endured during those years. Anchorage's role in the war continues to evoke pride among its residents, echoing the resilience and determination that shaped the era.

Conclusion

Beyond its scenic splendor and modern urban experiences, Anchorage conceals an unsung historical chapter of World War II. Anchorage's pivotal position, its role in the Alaskan Highway, military installations, and the resolute spirit of its inhabitants transformed it into an essential cog in the machinery of freedom and security. Anchorage's narrative in World War II echoes the enduring determination of a community that, while often overlooked, played a fundamental part in shaping the tapestry of history....

Modern Development and Urban Transformation

  - Anchorage, Alaska, a city embraced by breathtaking wilderness, has undergone a fascinating journey of modern development and urban transformation. Its evolution from a humble tent city to a vibrant metropolis has been shaped by a delicate balance between urban growth and preservation of its natural beauty.

Historical Foundations:

Anchorage's story begins in 1915 when it was established as a tent city for workers on the Alaska Railroad. Over the decades, the city's role as a transportation hub and gateway to Alaska's wild landscapes drove its growth. The historic Fourth Avenue, once a bustling commercial district, is a testament to Anchorage's beginnings.

Urban Planning and Infrastructure:

As Anchorage expanded, urban planning and infrastructure development played crucial roles in shaping the city. Thoughtful zoning and city planning have helped maintain the city's distinctive character. Downtown Anchorage boasts a mix of modern skyscrapers alongside charming historical buildings, reflecting a blend of past and present.

Cultural Renaissance:

Anchorage's urban transformation extends to its cultural scene. The city has embraced its indigenous heritage and nurtured a thriving arts and culture community. The Alaska Native Heritage Center stands as a testament to preserving and celebrating native cultures. Art galleries, theaters, and festivals contribute to a dynamic cultural landscape.

Balancing Nature and Progress:

Anchorage's unique position between civilization and the untamed wilderness is a defining factor in its development. Striking this balance has been a priority, with efforts to minimize urban sprawl and preserve natural spaces. The Chugach State Park, accessible from the city, highlights the commitment to maintaining the region's pristine landscapes.

Sustainability and Innovation:

Modern development in Anchorage emphasizes sustainability and innovation. The city's commitment to reducing its carbon footprint is reflected in initiatives like bike-friendly infrastructure, renewable energy projects, and green building practices. Anchorage's modernity aligns with its responsibility toward the environment.

Economic Growth and Industry:

Anchorage's evolution has been influenced by its economic landscape. The city's growth has been driven by industries such as tourism, transportation, and natural resource development. Anchorage International Airport, a major global hub, has played a pivotal role in connecting the city to the world.

Diverse Neighborhoods:

The city's neighborhoods mirror its transformation. From the bustling downtown core to eclectic districts like Spenard, each neighborhood has a distinct personality. Anchorage's diversity is reflected not only in its demographics but also in the varied architecture and local businesses.

Civic Engagement and Community Spirit:

Anchorage's urban transformation has been guided by civic engagement and community spirit. The Anchorage Downtown Partnership, for example, fosters collaboration among businesses, residents, and government to enhance the downtown area's vitality.

Adapting to Change:

The recent global challenges, including the COVID-19 pandemic, have showcased Anchorage's resilience and adaptability. The city's response to these challenges underscores its commitment to maintaining its unique urban-nature balance while ensuring the well-being of its residents.

Looking Forward:

Anchorage's journey of modern development and urban transformation continues. The city's commitment to sustainable growth, cultural enrichment, and the preservation of its wilderness soul defines its direction. Anchorage stands as a testament to how a city can evolve without losing sight of its roots and natural essence.

As you explore Anchorage, you'll witness not only its contemporary urban landscape but also the threads that connect its history, culture, and natural surroundings. It's a city that harmonizes modernity and tradition, inviting you to experience its vibrant pulse while respecting the majesty of the wilderness that surrounds it.

Anchorage's Multifaceted Culture

Arts and Performing Spaces

Anchorage, Alaska, a place renowned for its rugged landscapes and outdoor adventures, has also cultivated a vibrant arts and cultural scene that mirrors the city's unique blend of urbanity and wilderness. This synthesis of creative expression and natural beauty is beautifully showcased through its diverse arts and performing spaces, each contributing to Anchorage's cultural tapestry.

Anchorage Museum:

The **Anchorage Museum** isn't just a repository of artifacts; it's a living testament to Alaska's history, artistry, and cultural evolution. Its exhibitions extend beyond the ordinary, bridging the gap between the past, present, and future of the state. From celebrating indigenous heritage to highlighting contemporary creativity, the museum serves as an enlightening journey into Alaska's complex identity.

Alaska Center for the Performing Arts:

At the **Alaska Center for the Performing Arts**, the city's artistic heartbeat resonates. This state-of-the-art complex houses multiple theaters, providing a stage for a myriad of performances that range from Broadway shows to ballet, opera, concerts, and theatrical productions. Anchorage's residents and visitors alike gather here to witness artistic brilliance amidst the striking architecture and cutting-edge facilities.

Cyrano's Theatre Company:

In the heart of Anchorage, **the Cyrano's Theatre Company** offers an intimate theatrical experience that tugs at the emotions and stimulates the mind. Nestled within a charming building, this theater doesn't shy away from provocative and thought-provoking productions. Its dedication to innovative storytelling and contemporary performances establishes it as a hidden gem in the city's artistic tapestry.

Bear Tooth Theatrepub:

Bear Tooth Theatrepub redefines the cinematic experience by intertwining film, dining, and community engagement. This innovative concept combines screenings of mainstream and indie films with a laid-back pub atmosphere. Savor a meal while watching a movie, and you'll find yourself in a space where art, entertainment, and camaraderie converge.

Alaska Native Heritage Center:

Anchorage's pride in its indigenous heritage is exemplified by **the Alaska Native Heritage**

Center, a living museum that opens doors to the vibrant cultures of Alaska's native peoples. Here, visitors can immerse themselves in immersive experiences that explore traditional arts, crafts, and performances. The center is a bridge connecting past traditions to contemporary understanding.

First Friday Art Walk:

Anchorage's artistic spirit comes alive on the **First Friday Art Walk**, a monthly celebration that unveils the city's creative pulse. Galleries and businesses open their doors on the first Friday of each month, inviting locals and visitors to explore visual and performing arts. It's a platform to engage with the local creative community and dive into the diverse artistic expressions of the city.

Performing Arts Organizations:

Anchorage thrives on its dynamic performing arts organizations. From the **Anchorage Symphony Orchestra** to the **Anchorage Opera,** these ensembles deliver performances that span the realms of classical music and opera, enriching the city's cultural offerings and fostering a deeper appreciation for the performing arts.

Street Murals and Public Art:

Artistry isn't confined to indoor spaces alone. Anchorage's streets become canvases for vibrant murals and public art installations that narrate stories, celebrate local identity, and infuse urban spaces with color and creativity. A leisurely stroll becomes a visual journey through the collective imagination of Anchorage's artists.

Native Dance Performances:

Native dance performances offer a glimpse into the captivating world of indigenous cultures. These mesmerizing displays of traditional dances provide insight into the spiritual and cultural heritage of Alaska's native communities. Festivals and cultural events become windows into a timeless artistic legacy.

Workshops and Studios:

For those seeking a hands-on artistic experience, Anchorage offers a spectrum of workshops and classes hosted by local artists and artisans. Learn traditional crafts, contemporary techniques, and creative skills, whether it's pottery, painting, carving, or other art forms that pique your interest.

In summation, Anchorage's arts and performing spaces provide a profound window into the city's essence. The marriage of contemporary galleries, indigenous traditions, immersive cultural experiences, and captivating performances complements Anchorage's natural grandeur. Through exploration of these spaces, you're invited to discover the soulful pulse of Anchorage's artistic spirit, fostering a deeper connection to its multifaceted identity.

Culinary Scene: From Seafood to Fusion

Anchorage, a city that bridges the gap between untamed wilderness and urban vibrancy, also boasts a culinary scene as diverse as its landscapes. From fresh seafood plucked from the nearby waters to innovative fusion dishes that reflect the city's multicultural influences, Anchorage's dining offerings are a true reflection of its unique character.

Seafood Extravaganza:

Anchorage is synonymous with exceptional seafood. With the cold waters of the Pacific at its doorstep, the city serves up a seafood extravaganza that's a treat for the senses. Feast on succulent Alaskan king crab, renowned for its sweet and tender meat. Dive into the richness of freshly caught salmon, whether grilled, smoked, or prepared as sushi-grade sashimi. Halibut, another local favorite, graces plates with its delicate flavor and flaky texture.

Indigenous Flavors:

Anchorage's indigenous heritage is celebrated in its cuisine. Native Alaskan ingredients and traditional preparation techniques infuse local dishes with a unique taste. Look for dishes like Akutaq, a dessert made with whipped animal fat, berries, and other ingredients, or try Fry Bread Tacos, where Native American fry bread serves as a canvas for delicious fillings.

International Fusion:

Anchorage's diverse population has contributed to a fusion of international flavors. The city's culinary landscape is dotted with restaurants offering creative and delicious dishes that blend global cuisines. Savor Asian-inspired seafood dishes, explore Mexican-Thai fusion, or indulge in Hawaiian-Japanese delights that are a testament to Anchorage's culinary experimentation.

Farmer's Markets and Artisanal Products:

Anchorage's farmers' markets are vibrant hubs of local produce, handmade crafts, and artisanal foods. Sample freshly baked goods, savor local cheeses, and explore unique jams and preserves. These markets are not just about food; they're a cultural experience that connects you with Anchorage's community and its commitment to fresh, locally sourced ingredients.

Food Trucks and Street Food:

Anchorage's food scene extends to its streets, with a plethora of food trucks offering diverse and delectable options. From reindeer sausage to gourmet grilled cheese sandwiches, these mobile eateries bring a unique twist to classic street food fare. It's an ideal way to grab a quick bite while exploring the city's attractions.

Craft Brews and Local Spirits:

The culinary journey in Anchorage extends to its beverages. The city's craft breweries offer a wide range of beer styles, from hoppy IPAs to rich stouts, often using local ingredients for a distinct Alaskan touch. Don't miss the opportunity to sample some of the finest locally distilled spirits, including vodkas, gins, and more.

Waterfront Dining:

As you relish your meals, take in the stunning waterfront views that Anchorage offers. Numerous restaurants and cafes provide the perfect setting to enjoy your culinary adventures against the backdrop of the Cook Inlet and Chugach Mountains.

Sustainability and Freshness:

Anchorage's commitment to sustainability shines through in its culinary choices. Many restaurants prioritize locally sourced ingredients, highlighting the freshest seasonal produce, seafood, and meats. This dedication to sustainability not only supports local producers but also ensures you're enjoying the highest quality dishes.

Experiencing Native Traditions:

Beyond the plate, immerse yourself in cultural experiences that delve into Native Alaskan traditions and cuisine. Participate in workshops, cooking classes, or events that offer insights into ancient preparation methods and the significance of food in indigenous culture.

Festival of Flavors:

Anchorage's culinary prowess is celebrated through events like the "Anchorage Restaurant Week" and various food festivals. These occasions showcase the city's gastronomic diversity, providing opportunities to taste a variety of dishes from different eateries all in one place.

In Anchorage, the culinary scene is an exploration of tradition, innovation, and fusion, mirroring the city's ability to blend nature with urban living. From the freshest seafood to inspired fusion creations, every bite tells a story of Anchorage's rich history and vibrant present. Whether you're a seafood enthusiast, an adventurous foodie, or simply looking for an authentic taste of Alaska, Anchorage's diverse and evolving culinary landscape is sure to satisfy every palate.

Festivals and Celebrations

Anchorage, Alaska, transcends being a mere destination for natural beauty and outdoor adventures. It pulsates with a dynamic festival scene that reflects the city's cultural diversity, historical significance, and exuberant spirit. These festivals are more than just events; they are gateways to Anchorage's soul, offering visitors a chance to connect with its rich tapestry of traditions, artistry, and collective joy.

Fur Rendezvous (Fur Rondy):

In the heart of winter, Anchorage pays homage to its fur-trading past with the Fur Rendezvous in February. This vibrant carnival takes you on a journey through time, as the city transforms into a wonderland of activities. Admire intricate snow sculptures, feel the rush of sled dog races, and chuckle at the whimsy of snowshoe softball. The highlight is the Running of the Reindeer, where brave souls dash alongside these majestic creatures, embodying the city's unique blend of history and merriment.

Anchorage International Film Festival:

As December unfolds, cinephiles descend upon Anchorage for the Anchorage International Film Festival. A celebration of global cinematic artistry, this event brings together filmmakers and movie enthusiasts alike. The festival screens an array of films, including documentaries that provoke thought, animations that inspire wonder, and short films that pack powerful narratives. It's a chance to immerse yourself in storytelling from diverse corners of the world.

Summer Solstice Festival:

With the "midnight sun" gracing Anchorage's skies in June, the city hosts the Summer Solstice Festival. This gathering captures the essence of communal spirit and the love for the outdoors. Live music reverberates through the streets, food vendors offer delectable treats, art exhibitions showcase local talent, and families revel in a plethora of activities. The festival embodies the city's appreciation for nature's bounty and the joy of shared moments.

Girdwood Forest Fair:

A short jaunt from Anchorage leads to the enchanting town of Girdwood, home to the Girdwood Forest Fair in July. Against the backdrop of the Chugach Mountains, this whimsical fair captures the essence of Alaskan creativity. Local artists and artisans showcase their crafts, musicians fill the air with melodies, and a sense of wonder envelops attendees. It's a chance to witness the authentic spirit of Alaskan creativity in a picturesque setting.

Alaska State Fair:

August brings the Alaska State Fair to nearby Palmer, drawing people from across the state to partake in a celebration of agriculture, arts, and entertainment. It's a culmination of Alaskan culture, featuring colossal vegetables, craft exhibitions, live concerts that reverberate through the air, and a jubilant carnival atmosphere. The fair offers a glimpse into the state's diverse talents and treasures.

Alaska Native Heritage Center Celebrations:

Throughout the year, the Alaska Native Heritage Center opens its doors to various cultural celebrations, offering insights into the traditions and lifestyles of Alaska's indigenous communities. These gatherings provide an opportunity to engage with native artistry, music, dance, and stories directly from those who have preserved these heritage-rich elements for generations.

Fourth of July Celebration:

Independence Day in Anchorage is a vibrant display of patriotism and camaraderie. Fireworks illuminate the night sky, and the city comes alive with parades, events, and live performances that celebrate the nation's freedom. Anchorage's locals and visitors join together in the spirit of unity and celebration.

Indigenous Peoples Day Celebration:

October sees Anchorage honoring Indigenous Peoples Day, a time to pay homage to Alaska's native communities. The celebration encompasses cultural performances that resonate with tradition, enlightening workshops, captivating storytelling, and a concerted effort to foster understanding and appreciation of native heritage.

Halloween Trick or Treat Street:

October also brings Halloween to Anchorage, where families can participate in the Trick or Treat Street event. Downtown businesses welcome costumed children to collect treats, creating a safe and festive environment for young and old to enjoy.

Winter Celebrations and Markets:

As winter settles in, Anchorage's festive spirit ignites with holiday markets, Christmas tree lighting ceremonies, and enchanting winter-themed events. The city's streets become illuminated with lights and decorations, enveloping residents and visitors alike in a magical atmosphere of seasonal joy.

Anchorage's festivals and celebrations are a window into its heart and soul. By aligning your visit with these events, you'll not only immerse yourself in Alaska's natural allure but also forge connections with its vibrant culture and tight-knit community. Anchorage doesn't just offer a journey through landscapes; it's an invitation to celebrate life, history, and the collective spirit that makes this city a true gem.

Exploring Anchorage's Neighborhoods

Downtown: Urban Heartbeat

Downtown Anchorage is the pulsating core of Alaska's largest city, where the harmony of urban living seamlessly melds with the breathtaking natural landscapes that surround it. This vibrant district serves as a hub for culture, commerce, entertainment, and community life, offering visitors a captivating blend of local flavor and cosmopolitan charm.

Cityscape and Architecture:

In the heart of Alaska's largest city, downtown Anchorage stands as a testament to the city's evolution, a landscape where modern architectural marvels coexist harmoniously with historically significant landmarks. The city's skyline showcases the progress Anchorage has made, from towering skyscrapers that touch the sky to charmingly preserved buildings that whisper tales of its past.

Cultural Attractions:

Downtown Anchorage beckons culture enthusiasts with open arms. At the Anchorage Museum, a contemporary masterpiece, the essence of Alaska's art, history, and indigenous heritage are displayed in a captivating fusion of exhibits. Here, you can

69

delve into the narrative of Alaska's past, explore its present, and gain insights into its ever-evolving future. Meanwhile, the Alaska Center for the Performing Arts ignites the city with the arts, hosting theater productions, musical performances, and artistic events that mirror the diversity and creativity of Anchorage.

Retail Therapy and Dining:

Downtown pulses with energy, an effervescent district that caters to the senses. From local boutiques offering handmade treasures to international brands, the shopping scene is a vibrant tapestry of tastes and styles. Anchorage's culinary scene is equally enticing, weaving together a myriad of flavors. Walk the streets and you'll find eateries, cafes, and restaurants serving everything from the freshest Alaskan seafood to global gastronomic delights, creating a symphony of flavors that resonates with every palate.

Festivals and Events:

Downtown Anchorage transforms into a hub of celebration during festivals and events, a stage where the city and its visitors come together in joyous harmony. The Fur Rendezvous Winter Festival, a cherished tradition since 1935, breathes life into winter with activities ranging from the exhilarating rush of dog sledding to the enchanting artistry of snow sculptures. When summer graces the city, the Anchorage Market and Festival paints the streets with vibrant colors. Here, you can savor local delicacies, explore unique arts and crafts, and immerse yourself in the city's lively spirit.

Outdoor Spaces:

Even amid the urban hustle, downtown Anchorage pays homage to its natural roots. Town Square Park, an oasis of green, invites moments of relaxation and community gatherings, creating a sanctuary within the city. The Tony Knowles Coastal Trail, starting from downtown, is a waterfront pathway that beckons walkers, runners, and cyclists. Along this trail, you can embrace the tranquility of the sea, witness wildlife in their natural habitats, and be captivated by breathtaking vistas that remind you of the surrounding wilderness.

Nightlife and Entertainment:

As the sun makes its descent, downtown Anchorage refuses to slumber. The vibrancy takes on a new dimension as bars, pubs, and music venues come alive with the rhythm of live performances and local bands. The night is yours to revel in, whether you're seeking a cozy evening of conversation or a night of dancing and excitement.

Community Engagement:

Downtown Anchorage isn't just a haven for tourists; it's the lifeblood of the local community. Farmers' markets and art walks create an inviting atmosphere of inclusivity, allowing visitors to engage with the heart and soul of the city. Anchorage's residents extend their warmth, sharing stories, traditions, and that indomitable Alaskan spirit.

Accessibility and Transportation:

Navigating downtown Anchorage is a breeze, a seamless blend of convenience and accessibility. The compact layout lends itself to exploration by foot, inviting leisurely strolls through its dynamic streets. Bike lanes cater to cyclists, enhancing the experience of discovery. For those seeking broader exploration, public transportation options like buses and trolleys provide easy access to major attractions, seamlessly connecting you to experiences both within and beyond the city's heart.

Conclusion:

Downtown Anchorage pulsates with life, embodying the convergence of urban vibrancy and the untouched beauty of nature. Its cultural treasures, commercial vitality, and the mesmerizing backdrop of the Chugach Mountains weave together a tapestry that encapsulates Anchorage's unique identity. Whether you're enticed by its cultural tapestry, culinary delights, or the promise of experiencing city life intertwined with wilderness adventures just a stone's throw away, downtown Anchorage stands ready to offer an unforgettable journey through Alaska's urban gem.

Midtown: Where Tradition Meets Modernity

Midtown Anchorage strikes a delicate balance between honoring time-honored traditions and embracing the pulse of modernity. Nestled between the rugged Alaskan wilderness and the dynamic downtown core, this district offers a captivating blend of cultural richness, contemporary amenities, and a sense of community that resonates with both locals and visitors.

Cultural Heritage and Architecture:

In the heart of Midtown Anchorage, the urban tapestry is interwoven with historical threads and modern fibers. Architectural diversity becomes a canvas for the district's identity, reflecting the passage of time and the evolution of a community. The juxtaposition of enduring structures and contemporary designs paints a vivid narrative of the district's journey through the ages.

Retail and Shopping:

Midtown's streets are a vibrant runway of shopping possibilities. Anchored by modern malls and charming boutiques, the district bridges the gap between global brands and local craftsmanship. Whether you're in pursuit of fashion trends, indigenous artifacts, or gear for your Alaskan escapades, Midtown's shopping scene caters to every curiosity.

Culinary Melting Pot:

Midtown Anchorage's culinary scene echoes its diverse populace. An array of flavors from around the world find their way onto plates here. Alaskan seafood mingles with global gastronomy, and local bistros coexist with international eateries. It's a culinary symphony where cultural harmony is served with every dish.

Cultural Exploration and Museums:

Midtown serves as a cultural gateway, inviting visitors to delve into the rich tapestry of Alaskan heritage. The Alaska Native Heritage Center, a luminary of Midtown's cultural landscape, immerses you in the stories of indigenous communities. The past comes alive through artistry, traditions, and historical narratives, fostering a deeper understanding of the region's roots.

Parks and Urban Retreats:

Midtown acknowledges the importance of green spaces in urban living. Parks like Cuddy Family Midtown Park provide a serene haven, where city dwellers can unwind, picnic, and forge connections with neighbors. Amid the bustle, these green oases offer a gentle reminder of Anchorage's natural pulse.

Business Pulse and Innovation:

Midtown Anchorage is not just a space of historical resonance; it's a driving force in the city's modern economy. It houses the heartbeats of corporations, medical institutions, and professional services, a testament to Anchorage's role as a commercial nucleus in the region.

Community Bonding:

Midtown fosters a sense of belonging that transcends generations. Festivals and markets bring people together, celebrating the spirit of unity that's deeply ingrained in the district's essence. Cultural events and communal gatherings create spaces where residents and visitors become part of the vibrant Midtown tapestry.

Modern Comforts and Infrastructure:

Rooted in tradition, Midtown Anchorage is not left behind in the wake of progress. It's a district where modernity intertwines seamlessly with tradition. Contemporary amenities ensure the comfort and convenience of residents and visitors alike, affirming the district's commitment to a harmonious urban lifestyle.

Nature's Embrace:

The allure of Alaska's wilderness is never far away, even within the heart of Midtown. With the majestic Chugach Mountains as a backdrop and easy access to outdoor adventures, the district encapsulates the natural spirit that courses through the veins of Anchorage.

In Conclusion:

Midtown Anchorage stands as a living embodiment of the delicate dance between tradition and innovation. It captures the district's ability to preserve its roots while embracing the dynamism of contemporary living. In Midtown, the echoes of the past mingle with the aspirations of the future, creating a symphony that beckons exploration, connection, and an appreciation for the indomitable spirit of Alaska.

Spenard: Quirky Creativity

Nestled within the heart of Anchorage, Spenard emerges as a neighborhood that radiates a distinctive charm and an unapologetic embrace of creativity. Known for its eclectic spirit and vibrant arts scene, Spenard is a canvas where the unconventional is celebrated, and the boundary between art and everyday life blurs.

Artistic Vibes:

Spenard is a sanctuary where artistic souls find solace. Walk down its streets, and you'll be immersed in a living art gallery. Colorful murals and vibrant graffiti adorn seemingly mundane walls, transforming them into thought-provoking canvases. Every corner tells a visual story, inviting passersby to pause and reflect. This is a neighborhood that doesn't just consume art—it exudes it. Art galleries, studios, and unconventional spaces breathe with life, hosting exhibits, performances, and installations that challenge norms and ignite conversations. The very essence of Spenard is woven with creative energy, a tapestry that evolves with every brushstroke and expression.

Local Establishments:

Spenard's artistic pulse extends to its local businesses. Quirky coffee shops welcome patrons with mismatched furniture and walls lined with local artwork. Independent bookstores invite literary exploration, each shelf a trove of hidden treasures waiting to be discovered. Unconventional boutiques beckon with unique finds, reflecting the neighborhood's spirit of individuality. Even eateries embrace innovation, serving up fusion flavors that tantalize taste buds and expand culinary horizons. Spenard's local scene isn't just about commerce—it's about curating an experience that resonates with the neighborhood's creative heartbeat.

Music and Entertainment:

Spenard's musical notes reverberate through its streets, forming a symphony that captivates all who listen. Live performances and open mic nights are the pulse of the community, where local talents take center stage. The neighborhood's venues play host to a diverse array of musical genres, offering a spectrum of experiences. As you step into Spenard's music scene, you'll find yourself in the midst of a soulful dialogue between artists and their audience. The energy is palpable, drawing both locals and visitors to partake in the magic.

Cultural Festivals:

Spenard comes alive during cultural celebrations that unite its residents. The Spenard Jazz Fest weaves enchanting melodies into the air, inviting everyone to sway to the rhythm of life. The Fools' Run, with its whimsical spirit, celebrates individuality and camaraderie as participants embrace eccentricity while running through the neighborhood's streets. These festivals serve as testament to Spenard's commitment to embracing diversity and celebrating the beauty of artistic expression.

Quaint Theatres and Performance Spaces:

The neighborhood's intimate theatres and performance spaces are incubators of innovation. Here, artists experiment with avant-garde productions, push boundaries with experimental plays, and invite audiences to embrace new perspectives. Spenard nurtures local talent, encouraging performers to take bold steps and explore uncharted territories. The neighborhood's stages are a playground for creativity, where imagination knows no bounds.

Alternative Spirit:

Spenard's alternative soul thrives through its unconventional offerings. Vintage shops offer a journey back in time, where treasures from decades past find new owners. Thrift stores are treasure troves of surprises, each item telling a unique story. Unconventional fashion statements challenge norms and invite self-expression. The neighborhood's embrace of the alternative extends to its residents, making Spenard a haven where everyone's individuality is cherished.

Community Art Projects:

Spenard's streets become stages for community-driven art projects that bring residents together. Initiatives like street clean-up campaigns transform ordinary objects into vibrant works of art, infusing life into the everyday. Collaborative murals narrate the neighborhood's history and aspirations, becoming a shared canvas that fosters a sense of togetherness and pride.

Quirky Landmarks:

Spenard's landmarks are symbols of its character. The "Spenard Welcome Arch," an iconic structure, is a testament to the neighborhood's creativity and eccentricity. Pass beneath it, and you're welcomed into a world where boundaries are fluid, and artistic expression knows no limits.

Conclusion:

Spenard isn't just a neighborhood; it's an ode to the unconventionality that resides within all of us. It's a place where walls speak stories, local businesses are curated experiences, and creativity pulses in the air. Spenard beckons those who seek more from life, inviting them to step beyond the ordinary and embrace the unexpected. Here, norms are questioned, and artistic souls are set free to explore uncharted territories. As you immerse yourself in Spenard's atmosphere, you'll discover that it's not just a place—it's an invitation to unleash your quirky creativity and revel in the joy of expression.

Mountain View: Community and Change

Nestled in the heart of Anchorage, Mountain View stands as a testament to the evolution of urban neighborhoods and the resilience of communities. This neighborhood, with its rich history and dynamic present, encapsulates the essence of Anchorage's diverse identity, offering visitors a glimpse into the tapestry of local life and the forces of change that shape it.

Mountain View serves as a vibrant microcosm within Anchorage's cultural mosaic, embodying the richness of diversity. This neighborhood thrives as a tapestry woven with threads of various cultures, languages, and traditions. Within its streets, visitors encounter a living symphony of humanity, where different stories converge to create a harmonious whole. The genuine warmth and welcoming atmosphere invite visitors to immerse themselves in the community's essence, encouraging dialogue, understanding, and the sharing of experiences that bridge the gaps between backgrounds.

Transformation and Revitalization:

Mountain View's evolution reflects the city's heartbeat and the trajectory of urban development. Its history, from its origins as a military housing area during World War II to its dynamic growth and challenges, embodies the journey of revitalization. Today, the neighborhood stands as a living testament to the balance between honoring its heritage and embracing the winds of progress. The past and present intertwine in the streets, showcasing a resilient community that embraces change while cherishing its roots.

Cultural Enclaves:

At the heart of Mountain View lies a vibrant spectrum of cultural enclaves. Markets, restaurants, and shops reflect the diverse heritage of its residents. Wander through the neighborhood, and you'll encounter the aromas of African, Latin American, Asian, and Pacific Islander cuisines, inviting you to embark on a culinary journey around the world. The businesses here are more than commercial ventures; they are gateways to understanding the lives and stories of those who call this place home.

Community Initiatives and Connection:

Mountain View's pulse beats strongly through community initiatives. Local organizations, centers, and gathering spaces serve as anchors for unity and empowerment. These spaces are more than physical; they are wellsprings of connection that empower residents to engage in education, art, and social activities that foster camaraderie. Within these spaces, the vibrancy of Mountain View's spirit comes to life as residents come together to create, learn, and grow.

Challenges and Progress:

Urban neighborhoods inevitably face challenges, and Mountain View is no exception. Confronting economic disparities, addressing affordable housing needs, and navigating social issues form part of the community's ongoing journey. Yet, the neighborhood's determination and collective efforts to tackle these challenges highlight its strength and commitment to driving positive change.

Cultural Celebrations and Festivals:

Mountain View pulses with energy during cultural celebrations and festivals. These events shine a spotlight on the neighborhood's diverse roots. From festivals that honor cultures from around the world to local showcases of talent and creativity, the streets come alive with the vibrant energy of communal celebrations. Visitors are invited to join in, engaging with the heart and soul of the neighborhood.

Public Art and Expression:

Mountain View's walls and spaces are adorned with art that speaks to the soul of the community. Murals, sculptures, and creative installations are more than decorations; they are expressions of identity, unity, and transformation. These art pieces share stories of the neighborhood's past, present, and aspirations, inviting passersby to pause, contemplate, and connect.

Future Aspirations:

Mountain View's path forward is one defined by aspiration and unity. The neighborhood continues to evolve, blending preservation with progress. Collaborative endeavors between residents, local authorities, and organizations pave the way for a future that is inclusive, thriving, and dynamic. Mountain View is not just a place; it's a vision of what a community can achieve through collective determination.

Engaging with the Community:

Visitors have a unique chance to become a part of Mountain View's story. By participating in cultural events, exploring local businesses, and interacting with residents, visitors gain a profound understanding of the neighborhood's heartbeat.

Engaging with the community fosters connections, breaks down barriers, and nurtures the spirit of unity that defines Mountain View.

Conclusion:

Mountain View stands as a living embodiment of transformation, diversity, and the enduring power of community. Anchorage's global heritage comes alive in the streets of this neighborhood, where unity and change coexist harmoniously. As visitors journey through Mountain View's streets, they embark on an exploration of communal bonds and the boundless potential for growth, offering a window into the ever-evolving identity of Anchorage.

Anchorage Outdoors
Anchorage's Natural Playground

In the heart of Alaska, where nature's grandeur reigns supreme, lies Anchorage—an urban haven intricately woven into a landscape that embodies the untamed beauty of the wild. Anchorage's natural playground is a symphony of rugged mountains, sprawling forests, crystalline waters, and the untethered spirit of adventure that invites both explorers and dreamers to embark on a journey of a lifetime.

Mountain Majesty: Chugach Range

Anchorage's backdrop is painted with the majestic strokes of the Chugach Range, a sprawling wilderness that serves as both a sanctuary and a challenge for those who seek elevation. Trekking enthusiasts traverse the slopes, ascending peaks that offer panoramic views of the city and beyond. The allure of the mountains is not limited to the brave—the surrounding valleys, adorned with alpine meadows and pristine lakes, invite leisurely strolls and introspective moments of connection with nature.

Alaska's Coastal Gem: Turnagain Arm

Turnagain Arm, a breathtaking fjord-like body of water, cradles Anchorage in its azure embrace. The shimmering waters are a testament to the delicate dance between land and sea—a place where the wilderness meets the tide. The arm is famed for its bore tide, an awe-inspiring natural phenomenon that surges through the inlet with the force of a river, drawing thrill-seekers to witness nature's grand spectacle.

Where Glaciers Glisten: Portage Glacier

Venturing beyond the city limits leads to the ethereal world of Portage Glacier—a monumental river of ice that encapsulates the mystique of the Alaskan wilderness. Embarking on a glacier cruise or hiking through the surrounding trails offers an intimate encounter with these colossal ice masses. The glacier's ethereal blue hues, the gentle creaking of ice, and the echoes of centuries past create an ambiance of timelessness that leaves an indelible mark on every visitor.

Wildlife Wonderland: Anchorage's Inhabitants

Anchorage's natural playground extends beyond landscapes to the creatures that call this wilderness home. It's a place where encounters with moose are as common as meetings with neighbors, where bald eagles perch majestically against the skyline, and where bears roam the outskirts, embodying the spirit of untamed nature. Anchorage's urban and wild boundaries intertwine, allowing residents and visitors to witness wildlife in their natural habitats with awe and respect.

City Meets Coastal: Kincaid Park

Kincaid Park, a haven of natural beauty nestled within the city's embrace, is a living testament to Anchorage's harmonious coexistence with the wild. Trails wind through old-growth forests, revealing vistas that stretch from the city skyline to the endless horizon of the sea. In winter, the park transforms into a snowy wonderland, inviting cross-country skiers and mushers to traverse its pristine paths.

In the symphony of Anchorage's natural playground, adventure awaits at every turn, and reverence for the wild is a prevailing sentiment. Here, the untamed wilderness is not a distant realm—it's an integral part of the city's essence, shaping the lives of its inhabitants and inviting explorers from around the world to discover the beauty, resilience, and wonder that thrive in the heart of Alaska's urban gem.

Hiking and Biking Trails

Nestled amidst the rugged landscapes and enveloped by the mesmerizing allure of the great outdoors, Anchorage, Alaska emerges as a haven for enthusiasts seeking to traverse the wilderness on two wheels or on foot. As the cityscape gives way to expansive trails and vistas, the heart of every adventurer finds a rhythm that resonates with the primal beauty of the land. Anchorage's hiking and biking trails offer a tapestry of experiences, where every step or pedal stroke becomes a moment of communion with nature's grandeur.

Flattop Mountain Trail: Ascend to the Skyline of Adventure

The Flattop Mountain Trail stands as a sentinel, inviting hikers to ascend its slopes and reach a vantage point that unveils the city's panorama against the backdrop of the Chugach Mountains. The journey is one of gradual elevation, where anticipation mounts with every step. As the summit is conquered, a breathtaking spectacle unfolds—a patchwork of urbanity juxtaposed with untamed wilderness. For mountain biking enthusiasts, the Flattop Mountain Trail offers a thrilling challenge, where technical skill meets the rugged terrain of the Alaskan frontier.

Tony Knowles Coastal Trail: A Symphony Along the Water's Edge

The Tony Knowles Coastal Trail, a masterpiece of design and nature's grandeur, stretches serenely along the coastline, offering both hikers and bikers an intimate dialogue with Anchorage's maritime beauty. With each mile, the trail unveils ever-changing vistas—the sparkling waters of Cook Inlet, the majesty of Denali on clear days, and the untamed foliage that thrives along the path. As bikers pedal with the ocean breeze in their hair and hikers saunter amidst the tranquility, the trail paints an unforgettable symphony of sights and sounds.

Kincaid Park: A Verdant Haven of Exploration

Kincaid Park, an expansive sanctuary within the city's embrace, unveils a tapestry of trails that cater to both hikers and mountain bikers. The park's trails wind through dense forests, revealing glimpses of the rugged coastline and the elusive wildlife that calls this wilderness home. For bikers, Kincaid Park offers a network of trails that range from leisurely paths to challenging single tracks, ensuring an adventure suited for all skill levels.

Powerline Pass Trail: A Wilderness Odyssey

As the cityscape recedes, the Powerline Pass Trail beckons with promises of a genuine wilderness odyssey. Hikers and mountain bikers traverse through the Chugach Mountains, where lush alpine meadows unfold against a backdrop of towering peaks. The trail's ruggedness becomes a testament to the untamed beauty of Alaska's backcountry, and each mile conquered becomes a badge of honor for adventurers seeking to embrace nature at its rawest.

Hillside Trails: Elevate Your Perspective

The Hillside Trail System, a treasure trove for both hikers and bikers, offers a multitude of paths that elevate explorers to new perspectives. The trail system offers a diverse range of experiences, from leisurely strolls amidst meadows adorned with wildflowers to challenging ascents that reward with panoramic views. As the sun's embrace touches the horizon, the Hillside Trails become a canvas of colors—a testament to the union of nature's brilliance and the human spirit's yearning for discovery.

In Anchorage, the trails become more than mere routes; they are stories waiting to be lived, moments etched in memory, and a dialogue with the wilderness that rejuvenates the soul. Whether you're seeking an adrenaline-fueled biking adventure or a meditative hike through serene landscapes, Anchorage's trails offer an invitation—an invitation to explore, to connect, and to immerse yourself in a world where the rhythm of your heart finds resonance with the pulse of the wild.

Wildlife Encounters and Bird Watching

. In the heart of Anchorage, a unique and captivating symphony of nature unfolds—a symphony orchestrated by the enchanting wildlife that call this Alaskan haven home. Anchorage, a city where urban and wilderness boundaries blur, offers an unparalleled opportunity for wildlife enthusiasts and avid bird watchers to immerse themselves in the rhythms of the wild.

Wildlife Encounters:

Anchorage's proximity to unspoiled wilderness creates an environment where wildlife encounters are not just possible but often a part of daily life. Imagine strolling through a park and suddenly crossing paths with a moose and her calf, or spotting a bald eagle majestically perched atop a tree as you explore the city's trails. Anchorage's unique geography, nestled between the Chugach Mountains and the ocean, provides a diverse habitat for various wildlife species.

The Tony Knowles Coastal Trail, a scenic pathway that winds along the coastline, offers an excellent chance to observe marine wildlife. Keep your eyes peeled for seals, otters, and even the occasional whale breaching in the shimmering waters of the Cook Inlet. For a more immersive experience, venture into Chugach State Park, where Dall sheep gracefully navigate the rugged slopes and black bears forage in their natural habitat.

Bird Watching:

Anchorage is a haven for bird watchers, offering a rich variety of avian species to admire. With over 300 species of birds recorded in the area, from migratory birds to year-round residents, the city presents an avian symphony that captivates both beginners and seasoned bird enthusiasts.

One of the city's most iconic bird species is the bald eagle, often seen soaring through the skies or perched near water bodies. The Alaska Botanical

Garden and the Anchorage Coastal Wildlife Refuge are prime locations to spot these majestic raptors. Meanwhile, Westchester Lagoon and Potter Marsh are popular spots to observe waterfowl, including trumpeter swans and northern pintails, against the backdrop of awe-inspiring Alaskan landscapes.

Responsible Wildlife Viewing:

While wildlife encounters can be thrilling, responsible viewing practices are paramount to preserving these precious creatures and their habitats. Keeping a safe distance, using binoculars or a camera with a telephoto lens, and minimizing disturbances are essential to ensure the well-being of both wildlife and visitors. Familiarize yourself with local guidelines for interacting with wildlife and always prioritize their comfort and safety.

Guided Tours and Educational Experiences:

For a deeper understanding of Anchorage's wildlife and avian diversity, consider joining guided tours and educational programs led by local experts. These excursions provide insights into the behaviors, habitats, and conservation efforts dedicated to the creatures that make Anchorage their home.

Educational Programs and Conservation Initiatives:

Anchorage's commitment to preserving its diverse wildlife is evident through its array of educational programs and conservation initiatives. The Alaska Wildlife Conservation Center, located just outside Anchorage, serves as a sanctuary for orphaned and injured animals, providing a unique opportunity to observe them up close while learning about their stories and the efforts to protect their species.

For those seeking a deeper immersion, the Alaska Zoo offers educational presentations that shed light on the behaviors, habitats, and conservation challenges faced by animals native to Alaska. These experiences not only enrich your understanding but also inspire a sense of responsibility towards protecting the delicate balance of nature.

Seasonal Highlights:

The rhythms of wildlife in Anchorage change with the seasons, offering a dynamic experience year-round. Spring witnesses the return of migratory birds, filling the skies with a cacophony of calls and vibrant plumage. Summer brings bustling activity as animals capitalize on the bountiful food sources. Fall's arrival is marked by the mesmerizing spectacle of salmon runs, where bears congregate along rivers to feast before hibernation. And even winter, with its snow-blanketed landscapes, showcases the resilience of creatures adapted to the Arctic environment.

Bird Watching Hotspots:

For avid bird watchers, Anchorage's diverse habitats provide an array of birding hotspots to explore. The Anchorage Coastal Wildlife Refuge, a haven for shorebirds, offers expansive tidal flats and marshes that attract a multitude of species. The Campbell Creek Estuary Natural Area provides a serene setting to observe waterfowl, sandpipers, and the elusive American bittern.

Venturing beyond the city, the Kenai Peninsula offers prime birding opportunities, including the chance to spot the endangered Kittlitz's murrelet and the elusive gyrfalcon. With its varied ecosystems, Anchorage and its surrounding areas offer an ever-changing canvas for birding enthusiasts to paint their ornithological adventures.

In conclusion, Anchorage's wild soul thrives harmoniously alongside its urban heartbeat, offering an unrivaled opportunity to witness nature's wonders up close. Whether you're captivated by the grace of a moose, the majesty of a bald eagle, or the melodious tunes of various bird species, Anchorage's wildlife encounters and bird watching experiences promise to be a symphony of emotions and discoveries that resonate deeply within the hearts of those who seek a genuine connection with the natural world.

Water Adventures: Kayaking, Fishing, and More

Nestled amidst the captivating Alaskan landscapes, Anchorage emerges as a haven for those seeking to immerse themselves in a world of aquatic wonders. Beyond its urban charms and natural splendors, the city's waterways offer a realm of exploration and adventure that beckons water enthusiasts from all corners of the globe. Whether you're drawn to the thrill of kayaking, the tranquility of fishing, or the allure of unique aquatic experiences, Anchorage's aquatic playground promises an unforgettable journey into the heart of the great outdoors.

Kayaking: Paddling through Pristine Beauty

Anchorage's surrounding waters are a mosaic of fjords, bays, and serene lakes, inviting adventurers to embark on kayaking expeditions that border on the magical. The sensation of gliding across mirror-like waters, surrounded by snow-capped peaks and lush wilderness, is nothing short of enchanting. Lake kayaking offers a tranquil escape, with the shimmering waters of Eklutna Lake and Kenai Lake inviting paddlers to bask in the serenity of their surroundings. For those seeking a more adventurous outing, coastal kayaking unveils the rugged beauty of Prince William Sound, where massive glaciers calve into the ocean and marine life thrives in abundance. Whether you're a seasoned kayaker or a novice eager to learn, Anchorage's diverse waterways promise a paddling experience that resonates deeply with nature's rhythms.

Fishing: Angler's Paradise

For those who find solace in the art of angling, Anchorage's fishing opportunities are nothing short of a dream. The city is a gateway to some of Alaska's most renowned fishing destinations, where salmon, trout, and a variety of other species abound. Cast your line in the mighty Kenai River, renowned for its trophy-sized salmon runs, or explore the clear waters of Ship Creek, nestled right in the heart of downtown Anchorage. In the warmer months, the city's rivers and lakes become a playground for both seasoned fishermen and newcomers, with the added delight of potentially witnessing the breathtaking phenomenon of the Northern Lights dancing overhead.

Unique Aquatic Experiences: Beyond the Ordinary

Anchorage's water adventures extend beyond traditional pursuits, inviting you to embrace the extraordinary. Dive into the world of paddleboarding, where you can navigate tranquil waters while standing atop a board, surrounded by nature's splendor. The thrill of gliding through the waves, occasionally spotting wildlife along the shores, makes for an unforgettable experience. For the truly daring, cold-water snorkeling allows you to explore Alaska's marine life up close, unveiling the mysteries of the underwater realm beneath the icy surface.

Guided Tours and Expertise

Embarking on these water adventures need not be a solitary endeavor. Anchorage offers a plethora of guided tours and outfitters, ensuring that both newcomers and experienced adventurers can delve into these activities with confidence. Seasoned guides share their expertise and local insights, enhancing your connection to the surrounding landscapes and wildlife.

Seasonal Variations

Anchorage's aquatic offerings transform with the seasons, each unveiling a distinct facet of its water wonders. Summer, with its longer days and milder temperatures, is prime time for kayaking, fishing, and paddleboarding. The lakes glisten under the sun's embrace, and the rivers are alive with the annual salmon runs—a spectacle that draws both anglers and observers alike. Spring and fall offer their own charm, with quieter waters and the added allure of vibrant foliage as the seasons transition.

Even in winter, Anchorage's aquatic playground doesn't rest. While kayaking may take a backseat, ice fishing becomes a cherished tradition. The city's frozen lakes and rivers become venues for drilling holes through the ice and patiently waiting for the fish to bite. It's an experience that captures the essence of Alaskan resilience and adaptability, reminding you that adventure knows no seasonal bounds.

So, as you prepare to embrace Anchorage's aquatic playground, let the waters carry you on a voyage of discovery. Whether you're seeking reflection, excitement, or a deeper understanding of Alaska's heart, the city's water adventures offer a canvas on which you can paint your own narrative—one stroke, one cast, and one memory at a time. Anchorage's waters await, inviting you to dive in and immerse yourself in an exploration that transcends the ordinary and captures the essence of the extraordinary.

Day Trips and Beyond
Chugach State Park: Wilderness Escapes

In the heart of bustling Anchorage lies a hidden gem—an expansive wilderness that beckons adventurers to step beyond the boundaries of urbanity and embrace the untamed beauty of nature. Chugach State Park, a colossal expanse of over half a million acres, stands as a testament to nature's grandeur, offering a sanctuary of unspoiled landscapes, rugged mountains, and pristine wilderness. As the city's skyline fades behind you, Chugach's majesty unfolds, inviting you to embark on a journey that bridges the gap between urban sophistication and the raw essence of the outdoors.

The Gateway to the Untamed:

Chugach State Park is not merely a destination; it's a gateway to an untamed realm that promises to transport you far from the urban landscape. As the city's rhythm fades, you're welcomed by nature's symphony—a harmonious blend of rustling leaves, babbling streams, and the distant calls of wildlife. This pristine wilderness is an immediate antidote to the everyday, a refuge where the soul finds solace.

Scenic Overload:

With each step deeper into Chugach's wilderness, you're greeted by a breathtaking panorama that stretches as far as the eye can see. The landscapes here are dynamic and diverse, ranging from alpine meadows adorned with vibrant wildflowers to towering glaciers that seem to touch the sky. Majestic mountains rise like sentinels, framing a canvas that shifts from serene lakes to craggy peaks with every turn.

Adventures for All:

Chugach State Park is a haven for outdoor enthusiasts of all levels. Trails crisscross the terrain, catering to both seasoned hikers and beginners looking for a leisurely stroll. For the intrepid explorer, summiting Flattop Mountain—an iconic peak—offers a challenge rewarded with panoramic views that stretch to the horizon. Cyclists, skiers, and snowshoers find their playground on the park's well-maintained trails, ensuring that Chugach's allure endures through every season.

A Haven for Wildlife:

Amidst the rugged landscapes, Chugach State Park is teeming with wildlife. Moose graze in alpine meadows, their silhouettes painting a scene straight from a nature documentary. Bald eagles soar gracefully through the skies, while bears and foxes traverse the terrain in search of sustenance. In this living ecosystem, every encounter is a reminder of nature's delicate balance.

Jewels of Chugach:

Within the embrace of Chugach, two destinations stand out as jewels in the crown of this wilderness. Flattop Mountain, with its accessible trail and panoramic rewards, draws hikers and photographers alike. The Eagle River Nature Center, nestled in the heart of the park, serves as an educational hub, providing insights into the park's ecology and guiding adventurers toward their chosen paths.

Beyond Exploration:

Chugach State Park is not just a place to visit; it's an experience that resonates deeply within the soul. The park beckons you to reconnect with nature in its purest form, to leave behind the distractions of modern life and immerse yourself in the symphony of the wild. Whether you're capturing the hues of sunset on your camera, picnicking by a tranquil lake, or simply finding solace in the rustling of leaves, Chugach's embrace invites you to rediscover the rhythms of nature.

A Symphony of Seasons:

As the seasons unfold, Chugach State Park metamorphoses, each chapter revealing a different facet of its allure. Spring paints the landscape with a riot of wildflowers, while summer offers long days of exploration under the midnight sun. Fall transforms the forests into a mosaic of fiery hues, and winter blankets the land in pristine snow, offering opportunities for snowshoeing, skiing, and snowboarding. In every season, Chugach's beauty is a reminder that nature's artistry knows no bounds.

Reverie Amidst Reality:

As you return to Anchorage's urban embrace, the memories of Chugach State Park linger—a tapestry of moments woven into your being. The wilderness becomes more than a place visited; it becomes a sanctuary where the heart finds refuge. Chugach's allure transcends time, a constant reminder that the call of the wild is always answered, and that in nature's embrace, the soul finds its sanctuary. Chugach State Park isn't just a day trip; it's a timeless escape, a connection to a world unspoiled, and an invitation to experience the wild in its purest form.

Kenai Peninsula Excursion

In the heart of Alaska's urban gem, Anchorage, lies a gateway to a realm of untamed beauty and captivating wilderness—the Kenai Peninsula. As you venture beyond the city's boundaries, a world of awe-inspiring landscapes, diverse wildlife, and immersive outdoor experiences unfurls before you. The Kenai Peninsula Excursion is not merely a journey; it's an odyssey that transports you from urban sophistication to the untamed grandeur of Alaska's natural wonders.

Embrace of Nature's Majesty:

Leaving the city's skyline behind, you embark on a scenic drive that takes you through picturesque landscapes. The Kenai Peninsula's allure lies in its ability to seamlessly blend coastal panoramas, towering mountain ranges, and lush forests into a harmonious masterpiece. Every turn of the road reveals breathtaking vistas that beckon you to pause, absorb, and capture the essence of this unspoiled wilderness.

Resplendent Wildlife Encounters:

As you venture deeper into the Kenai Peninsula, you'll discover that this is a realm where encounters with wildlife are not just probable—they're almost inevitable. Keep your camera ready as you may spot majestic bald eagles soaring overhead, curious moose ambling through meadows, and even the occasional glimpse of a bear prowling in its natural habitat. This is nature's theater, where you're both spectator and participant.

The Charms of Coastal Life:

One of the Kenai Peninsula's jewels is the coastal town of Seward. Perched at the cusp of Resurrection Bay, Seward offers an opportunity to immerse yourself in maritime wonder. Board a boat and embark on a cruise that meanders past colossal glaciers, where nature's frozen sculptures calve into the sea with a resounding splash. Here, you'll bear witness to the grandeur of glaciers while the ocean breeze kisses your skin.

The Call of Adventure:

For those who seek more than just passive admiration, the Kenai Peninsula provides an array of outdoor activities that cater to adventurers of all kinds. Cast your fishing line into pristine rivers to test your angling skills against the renowned salmon runs. Lace up your hiking boots and set forth on trails that lead to alpine meadows, hidden lakes, and panoramic overlooks that paint the landscapes in hues of wonder.

A Culinary Journey:

As the sun dips below the horizon, you'll find yourself returning to the town of Kenai, where a culinary experience awaits. Here, the ocean's bounty transforms into a feast fit for epicures. The freshest catch graces your plate, each bite a tribute to the region's maritime heritage and the fusion of flavors that define Alaskan cuisine.

Retreat into the Starlit Canvas:

As the day's adventures come to an end, the Kenai Peninsula's magic doesn't wane with the setting sun. On clear nights, the skies become a canvas ablaze with the dance of the Northern Lights. With minimal light pollution, you'll have a front-row seat to witness nature's most captivating light show—a mesmerizing spectacle that transcends words and ignites a sense of wonder.

Ancestral Echoes:

Beyond its scenic beauty, the Kenai Peninsula is steeped in indigenous history and culture. Immerse yourself in the stories of the native peoples who have lived in harmony with these lands for generations. Learn about their traditions, artistry, and connection to the land—an enriching experience that adds depth to your journey.

Conservation and Stewardship:

As you explore the Kenai Peninsula's pristine wilderness, you become a part of its ongoing narrative of conservation and stewardship. Engage with local initiatives aimed at preserving the region's natural treasures for generations to come. From responsible wildlife observation to minimizing your ecological footprint, your actions contribute to the protection of this sanctuary.

In this journey, the Kenai Peninsula Excursion from Anchorage isn't just an escape—it's a revelation. It's a passage from the ordinary to the extraordinary, a narrative of nature's symphony conducted on the peninsula's grand stage. With each step you take, each vista you behold, and each wildlife encounter you embrace, you'll become a part of a story that's been unfolding for eons—a story where the Kenai Peninsula and its untamed beauty invite you to be a witness, a participant, and a steward of the natural world. As you return to Anchorage, you'll carry with you not only memories but also a profound connection to a wilderness that has touched your heart and stirred your soul.

Matanuska Glacier Exploration

Nestled in the pristine wilderness surrounding Anchorage lies a magnificent natural wonder that beckons adventurers and nature enthusiasts alike— the awe-inspiring Matanuska Glacier. This colossal mass of ancient ice stands as a testament to the Earth's enduring beauty, inviting intrepid souls to embark on an extraordinary journey of exploration and discovery.

A Glacial Marvel:

The Matanuska Glacier is not merely a geological formation; it's a living embodiment of Earth's history. Formed over thousands of years, this glacier boasts an impressive length of over 26 miles and spans more than four miles at its widest point. Its sheer scale is humbling, and its presence serves as a reminder of the planet's dynamic forces that have shaped the landscapes we know today.

Access to Untouched Beauty:

While the bustling city of Anchorage rests nearby, the Matanuska Glacier offers an escape to a world that seems untouched by time. A scenic drive through the Matanuska-Susitna Valley brings you to the very edge of this icy giant. The moment you step onto the glacier's surface, you're transported to a realm where silence is broken only by the crackling of ancient ice and the soft whispers of the wind.

A Guided Expedition:

Embarking on a guided expedition is the key to unlocking the glacier's secrets. Experienced guides, intimately familiar with the glacier's contours, lead adventurers on an immersive journey. With every step, you'll gain insights into its formation, the influence of climate on its ever-changing landscape, and the delicate equilibrium that exists between ice and the environment.

Glacial Spectacles:

The Matanuska Glacier is a living canvas upon which nature paints a spectacular display. Witness the phenomenon known as "blue ice," an ethereal shade caused by the ice's density and unique crystal structure that absorbs all colors of the spectrum except blue. As the sunlight dances upon the surface, the glacier's icy formations—seracs, crevasses, and ice caves—morph into surreal sculptures, providing a sensory feast for the eyes.

Nature's Classroom:

Walking upon the Matanuska Glacier isn't just an adventure; it's an educational journey through the annals of time. The glacier becomes a living textbook on glaciology, climate change, and the fragile ecosystems entwined with these icy behemoths. As you traverse its ancient surface, you'll find yourself in awe of the stories it has to tell—stories of millennia-long transformations.

Captivating Photography:

For photographers, the Matanuska Glacier is a playground of visual wonder. The interplay of sunlight and ice creates an ever-changing tableau of reflections, contrasts, and textures. Capture the glacier's raw essence—be it illuminated by the gentle hues of sunrise or draped in the ethereal light of the golden hour. Each photograph becomes a testament to the glacier's unique beauty and your connection with it.

A Humbling Experience:

Exploring the Matanuska Glacier transcends the realm of sightseeing; it's an immersive encounter that instills a sense of humility and wonder. Standing amidst towering ice formations, surrounded by the vast expanse of frozen history, you're reminded of the insignificance of individual existence in the grand scheme of the Earth's timeline.

In the heart of the Alaskan wilderness, the Matanuska Glacier extends an invitation—a chance to witness the magnificence of nature's craftsmanship and to stand humbled before its frozen beauty. This journey isn't a mere adventure; it's a profound experience that connects you to the legacy of our planet's icy past. So, step onto the glacier's surface, let its ancient ice weave its tales around you, and leave with a heart forever etched with the memory of this remarkable encounter.

Whittier and Prince William Sound Adventure

In the heart of Anchorage's captivating embrace lies a doorway to an aquatic wonderland, an adventure that beckons seekers of natural marvels and maritime magic—Whittier and the breathtaking expanse of Prince William Sound. This remote coastal haven, nestled within the embrace of Alaska's majestic landscapes, unveils a world where glaciers gleam like frozen sapphires, wildlife thrives in harmony, and the sea's embrace tells stories of ancient grandeur and timeless beauty.

Whittier: A Coastal Gem of Tranquility

Whittier, a charming enclave nestled at the base of the formidable Chugach Mountains, exudes a sense of enchanting seclusion. Its unique allure lies not only in its picturesque beauty but also in the fascinating journey to reach it. Anchorage's tunnel connection to Whittier—North America's longest combined vehicle-railroad tunnel—transforms the voyage into a mesmerizing transition from urban energy to coastal serenity.

The Intricate Tapestry of Prince William Sound

As one sets sail into the open expanse of Prince William Sound, a realm of wonder unravels. The sound's vastness is home to a multitude of islands, fjords, and coves, each concealing their own secrets and treasures. Here, the symphony of nature is composed of glistening glaciers, thriving marine life, and the serene expanse of azure waters—the canvas upon which every adventure is painted.

Dazzling Encounters with Glacial Giants

A voyage through Prince William Sound is a journey into the realm of glaciers—mighty rivers of ice that calve into the sea with an exhilarating spectacle. Stand in awe before the towering mass of Surprise Glacier, witness the ethereal beauty of Blackstone Glacier, and feel the reverberation of ice meeting water—an encounter that evokes profound respect for the earth's primal forces.

Kayaking: Paddling into Tranquility

For those seeking an intimate communion with the water, kayaking in Prince William Sound offers an unrivaled experience. Glide through still waters, your paddle breaking the mirrored surface as you navigate amidst ice floes and stunning fjords. The silence is punctuated by the sound of your strokes and the distant echoes of nature, creating an atmosphere of tranquil serenity.

Wildlife Ballet: An Awe-Inspiring Performance

Prince William Sound is a stage upon which nature's symphony is performed. Witness the choreography of orcas slicing through waves, sea otters playfully cavorting, and the grandeur of humpback whales breaching the surface—a spectacle that reminds us of the world's untamed beauty. The skies are alive with the balletic flight of seabirds, completing this masterpiece of living artistry.

The Return to Whittier: A Homeward Journey

As the sun dips below the horizon, your journey leads back to the welcoming shores of Whittier. The town's sense of community is palpable—a place where maritime heritage meets modern tranquility. As the lights twinkle in the evening sky, you're invited to relish the taste of locally caught seafood, sharing stories of the day's aquatic encounters with fellow travelers and kindred spirits.

A Timeless Tale of Prince William Sound

The symphony of Whittier and Prince William Sound orchestrates an unforgettable experience—a journey where nature's elegance and raw power merge to create an awe-inspiring tale. This aquatic adventure transcends the boundaries of mere travel; it's a narrative that intertwines with your soul, reminding you of the magic of exploration and the enduring connection we share with the natural world. So, as you venture into the enchantment of Whittier and Prince William Sound, embrace every moment as a chapter in a story that transcends time and leaves an indelible mark upon your heart.

Anchorage's Hidden Gems

Offbeat Attractions and Unique Finds

When journeying through Anchorage, Alaska, there's a special thrill in unearthing the lesser-known treasures that lie just beyond the well-trodden paths. While the city's natural wonders and iconic landmarks are awe-inspiring, its offbeat attractions and unique finds offer a chance to dive deeper into the heart and soul of this captivating destination. Embark on a journey of discovery as you explore Anchorage's hidden gems, each offering a distinct perspective and enriching your experience in unexpected ways.

Earthquake Park: Unveiling History's Echoes

In Earthquake Park, history whispers through the wind and rustling leaves. This serene park along the coastline stands as a testament to Anchorage's resilience in the face of nature's fury. The remnants of the 1964 earthquake, which reshaped the city's landscape, now tell a story of both destruction and rebirth. Walking the trails amid upturned trees and fractured ground, you can almost feel the tremors of the past, reminding us of the awe-inspiring power of our planet.

Anchorage Market and Festival: A Kaleidoscope of Culture

As the sun paints the sky with hues of dawn, the Anchorage Market and Festival comes alive. It's not just a market—it's a celebration of cultures, a melting pot of art, music, food, and community. With vendors showcasing their crafts, musicians serenading the crowd, and aromas of diverse cuisines mingling in the air, this gathering captures the heart of Anchorage's creative and welcoming spirit.

Imaginarium Discovery Center: Where Science Meets Play

For those who crave intellectual adventure, the Imaginarium Discovery Center is a haven of wonder. Step into a realm where scientific concepts are transformed into captivating experiences. Explore interactive exhibits that challenge your perceptions, and let the planetarium's celestial shows ignite your curiosity about the cosmos. It's a reminder that learning is an ever-evolving journey filled with joy and fascination.

The Ulu Factory: Crafting Tradition and Innovation

At The Ulu Factory, tradition meets innovation in the form of the ulu—an emblem of Eskimo culture. Watch as skilled artisans deftly shape these knives, preserving a heritage that spans generations.

Beyond the craft itself, you'll find ulu-inspired creations that bridge the gap between past and present, showcasing the enduring appeal of cultural heritage.

Ship Creek: Urban Angler's Paradise

While Anchorage's urban landscape might not immediately evoke images of fishing, Ship Creek challenges expectations. This hidden gem offers a unique angling experience within city limits. Join local enthusiasts casting their lines into the creek's waters, hoping to hook the mighty salmon that make their journey here. It's a chance to connect with nature, even amidst the city's hustle and bustle.

Alaska Aviation Museum: Wings of History

Lake Hood's shores cradle a treasure trove of aviation history—the Alaska Aviation Museum. Venture into the world of aviation pioneers, surrounded by vintage aircraft that once soared Alaska's skies. The museum's immersive exhibits and captivating stories encapsulate the vital role aviation has played in shaping the state's past and present.

Cyrano's Theatre Company: Intimate Theatrical Magic

For an evening of culture and connection, the cozy confines of Cyrano's Theatre Company beckon. Sit back and immerse yourself in performances that evoke emotion and provoke thought. The intimacy of the space creates a shared experience, where the lines between the stage and the audience blur, allowing for a deeper connection with the artistry.

Arctic Valley: Skiing with a View

Arctic Valley, a hidden gem among Anchorage's mountains, offers skiing with a panoramic twist. The slopes here come with more than just the thrill of skiing; they come with breathtaking vistas of the city and the surrounding landscape. Whether you're a seasoned skier or a novice, the opportunity to carve through powder while gazing upon Anchorage's splendor is an experience to treasure.

As you venture beyond the expected, Anchorage's offbeat attractions and unique finds provide a multi-dimensional view of the city's soul. They invite you to embrace the stories that are etched into its fabric, to connect with its creative pulse, and to discover the treasures that await those willing to seek them out. Anchorage's allure lies not just in its well-known features, but also in the intimacy of its hidden treasures that whisper of untold stories and authentic connections.

Local Markets and Craftsmanship

In the heart of Anchorage, a world of enchantment unfolds through its local markets and the intricate craftsmanship they proudly showcase. Beyond the glossy facades of modernity, these markets serve as gateways to the city's soul, offering visitors a chance to immerse themselves in the rich tapestry of Alaskan culture, creativity, and heritage. As you step into these bustling hubs, prepare to be transported to a realm where tradition and innovation harmonize to create an unforgettable sensory experience.

Cultural Kaleidoscope: Anchorage's Local Markets

Anchorage's local markets are a reflection of the city's diverse heritage, brimming with colors, aromas, and artifacts that narrate the stories of indigenous communities, settlers, and contemporary artisans. The markets are more than just commercial spaces—they're living repositories of culture, where age-old traditions find new expressions, and where visitors and locals converge to celebrate the spirit of Alaska.

Anchorage Market and Festival: Where Cultures Converge

At the heart of this cultural medley stands the Anchorage Market and Festival, a vibrant celebration that weaves together the threads of art, music, and culinary wonders. The market unfolds against the backdrop of the Chugach Mountains, creating a picturesque setting that enhances the allure of the bustling stalls. Here, local artisans proudly display their creations, offering everything from intricate handcrafted jewelry to unique woodwork and traditional Native Alaskan crafts.

Culinary Odyssey: A Gastronomic Affair

As you wander through the markets, your senses will be tantalized by the aroma of smoked salmon, the sizzle of reindeer sausages, and the delectable scent of freshly baked pastries. Anchorage's local markets are a haven for food enthusiasts, offering a chance to sample Alaskan delicacies and international flavors alike. From gourmet treats to organic produce, the markets provide a sumptuous palette of choices that cater to diverse tastes.

Craftsmanship Beyond Borders: Artisanal Elegance

The craftsmanship on display in Anchorage's markets is a testament to the city's devotion to preserving tradition while embracing innovation. Local artisans infuse their creations with a sense of pride and passion, weaving together the old and the new. Whether it's the intricate beadwork of indigenous artists, the elegance of hand-carved sculptures, or the contemporary designs of clothing and accessories, the markets are a gallery of human ingenuity.

Connecting with the Makers: A Personal Encounter

Beyond the allure of the products, Anchorage's local markets offer a unique opportunity to connect with the artisans themselves. Engaging in conversations with these creators provides insights into their creative processes, the stories behind their crafts, and a deeper appreciation for the artistry that defines their work. It's a chance to forge a personal connection, allowing you to carry a piece of their passion and authenticity home with you.

Sustaining Tradition, Empowering Communities

Visiting these local markets isn't just about acquiring souvenirs; it's about contributing to the sustenance of local economies and the preservation of cultural heritage. By supporting local artisans and craftsmen, you become a part of the ongoing narrative that keeps traditions alive and empowers communities to flourish.

In Conclusion

Anchorage's local markets are more than just shopping destinations; they're gateways to understanding, respect, and admiration for the city's intricate cultural fabric. From the intricate craftsmanship to the tantalizing flavors, each stall tells a story—an ode to the fusion of past and present, nature and creativity, tradition and innovation. Embark on a journey through these markets, and you'll find yourself not just buying products, but also immersing yourself in the vibrant heart of Anchorage.

Captivating Views: Scenic Points and Hidden Vistas

Anchorage, a city embraced by the rugged beauty of Alaska's wilderness, offers a visual symphony that resonates through its scenic points and hidden vistas. From sweeping panoramas that take your breath away to tucked-away gems that invite introspection, Anchorage unveils a captivating tapestry of natural wonders that leave an indelible mark on your soul.

Aerial Heights: Flattop Mountain

Perched at the city's edge, Flattop Mountain stands as a sentinel offering unparalleled vistas. As you ascend the trail, Anchorage's urban sprawl transforms into a mosaic of miniature buildings. The city's coastline embraces the azure waters of the Cook Inlet, and beyond, the Chugach Mountains rise majestically. The summit rewards your efforts with a 360-degree spectacle—the urban pulse blending seamlessly with the untamed wilderness.

Charm of the Coastal Trail: Earthquake Park

The Tony Knowles Coastal Trail is a sensory journey, and Earthquake Park is a hidden gem along this path. This serene spot commemorates the 1964 Good Friday Earthquake, and as you wander through its quiet pathways, the Anchorage skyline shares the stage with coastal wetlands, the distant Alaska Range, and the haunting beauty of the Northern Pacific Ocean. Sunset paints the sky with hues that match your sense of awe.

Wilderness and Reflection: Reflection Lake

For those yearning for serenity, Reflection Lake offers a serene escape. Nestled in the Chugach State Park, this mirror-like waterbody offers a pristine reflection of the world around it. The surrounding peaks, often capped with snow, stand mirrored in the tranquil waters, creating a surreal tableau that fosters contemplation and peace.

Majestic Peaks: Glen Alps Overlook

The Glen Alps Overlook is a testament to the grandeur of the Chugach Mountains. As you gaze upon the rugged peaks, a feeling of insignificance and reverence washes over you. Whether cloaked in winter's embrace or kissed by summer's light, the mountains form an awe-inspiring backdrop, reminding you of nature's boundless beauty.

Sensory Feast: Point Woronzof

At Point Woronzof, the sensory feast unfolds as the tides of the Cook Inlet meet the shore in a rhythmic dance. As you stand on the bluff, the salty breeze carries tales of distant lands, and the sight of Mount Susitna across the inlet evokes wonder. The transition of seasons paints the landscape with ever-changing hues, leaving an imprint of nature's dynamic artistry.

Hidden Treasures: Elderberry Park

Tucked away near downtown, Elderberry Park invites you to step into a world of tranquility. The serene waters of the Knik Arm glisten, and as the sun dips below the horizon, the city's lights begin to twinkle, creating a soothing ambiance. It's a reminder that beauty thrives not only in grand vistas but also in the moments of quiet contemplation.

As you traverse Anchorage's scenic points and uncover its hidden vistas, remember that this city's visual symphony transcends mere sightseeing. It's an invitation to connect with the primal rhythms of nature, to be humbled by its grandeur, and to find solace in its serenity. Anchorage's captivating views are a testament to the profound beauty that exists at the intersection of urbanity and untamed wilderness—a beauty that leaves an indelible imprint on your heart and soul.

Anchorage for Families and Solo Travelers

Family-Friendly Activities and Attractions

Anchorage, Alaska, isn't just a destination for intrepid adventurers; it's a treasure trove of experiences that cater to every member of the family. Amidst the breathtaking wilderness and cultural charm, this Alaskan gem offers an array of family-friendly activities and attractions that promise to create cherished memories for all ages.

Zoo Ventures and Wildlife Wonders:

For families seeking a wildlife immersion, the Alaska Zoo is a must-visit. Home to a diverse array of animals, from majestic moose to playful otters, the zoo provides an opportunity for kids to get up close and personal with native Alaskan creatures. Educational encounters and interactive exhibits transform learning into an exciting adventure.

Aviation Adventure at Lake Hood:

Fuel young imaginations at Lake Hood, the world's largest seaplane base. Watch as seaplanes gracefully glide onto the water, inspiring dreams of airborne exploration. Families can take guided tours, learn about the history of aviation, and even experience a thrilling seaplane ride—an experience that's bound to make hearts soar.

Immersive Learning at the Anchorage Museum:

Cultivate curiosity at the Anchorage Museum, a hub of art, history, and science. Engaging exhibits allow families to explore Alaska's heritage, delve into the mysteries of the universe, and unleash their creativity through interactive activities. The Thomas Planetarium is a starry haven for budding astronomers.

Trailblazing on the Tony Knowles Coastal Trail:

Nature-loving families will find solace on the Tony Knowles Coastal Trail. This paved pathway offers an easily navigable route for walking, biking, or rollerblading. Admire stunning views of the ocean and the Chugach Mountains as you meander along the shores of Cook Inlet, with opportunities to spot wildlife and enjoy picnics.

Captivating Performances at Cyrano's Theatre Company:

The magic of live theater comes alive at Cyrano's Theatre Company, where family-friendly productions whisk audiences away to enchanting worlds. From fairy tales to beloved classics, these performances captivate young minds and offer a chance for families to share the wonder of storytelling.

Cultural Exploration at the Alaska Native Heritage Center:

Enrich your family's understanding of Alaska's indigenous cultures at the Alaska Native Heritage Center. Engaging exhibits, storytelling sessions, and interactive demonstrations allow visitors to immerse themselves in the traditions, history, and artistry of Alaska's Native peoples.

Outdoor Adventures at Kincaid Park:

Kincaid Park, a vast natural playground, is a paradise for families seeking outdoor adventures. Whether it's hiking, biking, or simply exploring the rugged terrain, the park offers a chance for families to connect with nature and create lasting memories amidst the Alaskan wilderness.

Thrills and Learning at the Imaginarium Discovery Center:

Prepare for hands-on learning at the Imaginarium Discovery Center. This science-focused attraction features interactive exhibits that encourage exploration, experimentation, and a deeper understanding of the natural world. It's an ideal blend of education and fun for inquisitive young minds.

Delightful Waterfront Adventures at Ship Creek:

Fishing enthusiasts, both young and old, will relish the chance to cast a line into Ship Creek. This urban fishing spot offers a unique opportunity to catch salmon and learn about angling techniques. Guided tours and fishing equipment rentals make this experience accessible to families.

Winter Wonder at the Arctic Valley Ski Area:

When winter blankets Anchorage, families can embrace the snowy wonderland at the Arctic Valley Ski Area. With slopes catering to various skill levels and opportunities for skiing, snowboarding, and tubing, the whole family can revel in the joy of winter sports.

In Anchorage, the adventures are as diverse as the family members embarking on them. From encounters with wildlife to educational explorations and thrilling outdoor activities, the city's family-friendly attractions ensure that every moment spent together becomes a treasured chapter in your family's journey. Anchorage isn't just a destination—it's an invitation to create memories that will forever warm the hearts of young and old alike.

Practical Tips for Traveling with Children

Traveling with children requires meticulous planning and thoughtful preparation to ensure a smooth and enjoyable journey for the entire family. Anchorage, with its blend of urban charm and natural beauty, presents a unique backdrop for family adventures. To maximize your Anchorage experience while traveling with children, consider these expert tips for a seamless and enriching getaway:

Strategic Planning:

Advance preparation is key to a successful family trip. Research family-friendly activities, attractions, and accommodations in Anchorage. Tailor your itinerary to accommodate your children's interests, energy levels, and daily routines.

Dress Appropriately:

The Pacific Northwest climate can be unpredictable, so pack versatile clothing options that allow for layering. Ensure your children are dressed comfortably for outdoor exploration, with waterproof and wind-resistant outerwear for potential weather shifts.

Accommodation Selection:

Choose accommodations that cater to families. Many hotels and lodges in Anchorage provide amenities such as cribs, high chairs, and play areas, ensuring a comfortable and convenient stay for your family.

Health and Safety Essentials:

Prioritize your children's safety by carrying a well-stocked first aid kit, including essentials like adhesive bandages, antiseptic wipes, and any prescribed medications. Have their medical records and emergency contact information on hand.

Culinary Considerations:

Anchorage boasts a diverse culinary scene, but young palates can be selective. Seek out restaurants offering kid-friendly options or familiar cuisines, ensuring that dining experiences are enjoyable for everyone.

Enriching Attractions:

Anchorage features attractions designed to captivate young minds. Consider visiting the Alaska Zoo, where children can engage with diverse wildlife. The Alaska Aviation Museum and the Imaginarium Discovery Center offer interactive learning experiences suitable for all ages.

Parks and Recreation:

Allocate time for play at Anchorage's parks and playgrounds, providing children with spaces to burn energy and explore. Delaney Park Strip and Town Square Park are popular options within the city.

Wildlife Encounters:

Kids are often intrigued by wildlife. Visit the Alaska Wildlife Conservation Center, a safe environment where children can observe and learn about native animals up close, leaving them with lasting memories.

Family-Friendly Outdoor Ventures:

For older children, consider family-friendly outdoor activities such as hiking, biking, or kayaking. The Tony Knowles Coastal Trail, offering scenic waterfront views, is an ideal choice for leisurely walks or bike rides.

Cultivating Cultural Awareness:

Introduce your children to Alaska's indigenous cultures through visits to local museums and cultural centers. The Anchorage Museum features interactive exhibits and programs that engage young learners.

Prioritize Rest:

Children's energy levels vary throughout the day. Schedule breaks to allow for rest and relaxation, whether it's a leisurely picnic or a moment of tranquility in a park.

Educational Engagement:

Transform your Anchorage exploration into an educational journey. Share captivating insights about Alaska's history, geography, and wildlife, fostering curiosity and understanding.

Local Events and Celebrations:

Stay informed about local family-friendly events and festivals occurring during your visit. Anchorage often hosts cultural celebrations, art fairs, and outdoor festivities that offer unique engagement opportunities for children.

Flexibility is Key:

Acknowledge that children thrive in their own rhythms. Maintain flexibility in your plans, allowing room for spontaneity and adjustments based on your children's needs and interests.

Create Lasting Memories:

Capture the essence of your Anchorage adventure through a collective travel journal, where your children can jot down experiences, insights, and creative expressions. Document the journey with photographs that encapsulate the moments of joy and discovery.

By embracing these expert tips, your family journey to Anchorage can transform into an extraordinary and enriching experience. Anchorage's blend of cultural charm, natural marvels, and community warmth is poised to create unforgettable memories for both you and your children, fostering a bond that endures long after the adventure concludes.

Anchorage's Culinary Delights

Seafood Galore: From Salmon to King Crab

In the realm of culinary indulgence, Anchorage stands as a resplendent jewel, celebrated for its unparalleled bounty from the sea. A tantalizing canvas of flavors, textures, and gastronomic artistry, the city's dining scene is a veritable tapestry of seafood wonders that beckon connoisseurs from every corner of the world. Anchorage, Alaska—the epicenter of seafood abundance—invites you on a voyage of the palate, where the ocean's treasures are transformed into culinary masterpieces that are nothing short of awe-inspiring.

Sustaining Heritage, Elevating Flavor: Salmon's Ascendance

In the heart of Anchorage's gastronomic narrative, the salmon reigns supreme—a culinary heritage that runs as deep as the rivers from which it emerges. Anchorage boasts a unique connection with the salmon's lifecycle, as the city's landscape intertwines with the path of this remarkable fish. From the vibrant hues of sockeye to the robust flavors of king salmon, the city's eateries present a symphony of dishes that honor this noble fish. Grilled, smoked, or delicately cured, the salmon's versatility graces the tables of Anchorage, connecting diners to a tradition that encapsulates both sustenance and culture.

Culinary Royalty: The Alaskan King Crab

As the Alaskan seas yield their treasures, another regal protagonist graces Anchorage's dining scene—the majestic Alaskan king crab. With its colossal proportions and succulent meat, the king crab is a coveted gem that elevates seafood dining to a royal affair. From sumptuous crab legs bathed in clarified butter to intricate crab-filled pastries, Anchorage's culinary artisans pay homage to this crustacean monarch, transforming its essence into decadent creations that evoke both reverence and delight.

From Ocean to Plate: Anchorage's Maritime Playground

Anchorage's seafood epic showcases an array of marine marvels beyond the iconic salmon and king crab. Local markets and dining establishments present a cornucopia of treasures—from halibut and cod to spot prawns and scallops. Each delicacy offers a distinct expression of the ocean's generosity, prepared with culinary finesse that accentuates the innate flavors of the sea. Anchorage's chefs, often sourcing directly from local waters, exhibit an artisanal mastery that transforms each catch into an unparalleled dining experience.

Farm-to-Table Seafaring: Sustainability in Every Bite

In Anchorage, the relationship with seafood goes beyond mere consumption; it's an ethos that embraces sustainability and reverence for nature's provisions. Anchorage's commitment to responsible sourcing and eco-conscious practices ensures that every seafood encounter is an act of mindful indulgence. Whether you're savoring an innovative seafood fusion or a classic preparation, you're contributing to a gastronomic movement that safeguards the very ecosystems that birthed these culinary treasures.

A Symphony of Tastes: Anchorage's Seafood Odyssey

From upscale seafood bistros to unassuming waterfront eateries, Anchorage's culinary landscape offers a symphony of seafood experiences that cater to every palate and preference. Whether you're indulging in a thoughtfully crafted tasting menu or enjoying a casual seafood feast overlooking the waters that nurtured these flavors, Anchorage's seafood odyssey is a captivating journey that transcends mere nourishment.

In the realm of culinary artistry, Anchorage's seafood galore is a masterpiece—a testament to the symbiotic relationship between a city and its oceans. Anchorage invites you to embark on a culinary journey that spans the depths of the sea, celebrates tradition, and embraces innovation. From the first bite to the last, the flavors of Anchorage's seafood bounty leave an indelible mark on your palate, crafting an unforgettable chapter in your epicurean adventure.

International Flavors and Local Ingredients

In the heart of Anchorage, a culinary symphony unfolds—an exquisite orchestration of international flavors harmonizing with the bountiful offerings of the region's own terroir. Anchorage's gastronomic landscape is a reflection of its diverse populace and its commitment to embracing global influences while honoring the rich tapestry of local ingredients. Prepare to embark on a gastronomic odyssey through the city's eateries, where every plate is a canvas painted with the fusion of international culinary traditions and the essence of Alaska's natural bounty.

Anchorage's dining scene is a veritable kaleidoscope of cultures, each contributing its own hue to the city's culinary mosaic. Amidst the city's bustling streets, you'll discover a treasure trove of international cuisines, from Thai and Mexican to Japanese and Ethiopian. Each dish is a testament to the skill and passion of Anchorage's chefs, who weave their own interpretations of global classics with meticulous attention to detail.

Yet, it's not just the flavors of distant lands that grace Anchorage's tables; it's the symbiosis of these flavors with the region's indigenous ingredients that truly sets the city's culinary experience apart. The cold waters that cradle the city have nurtured a rich array of seafood, from succulent Alaskan king crab to pristine salmon that make their journey from the icy depths to the plate. Anchorage's chefs transform these treasures of the sea into culinary masterpieces that celebrate both the ocean's bounty and the artistry of their craft.

Venture into Anchorage's vibrant markets, where local artisans showcase their dedication to preserving the essence of Alaska's landscape. Freshly harvested vegetables, berries, and wild game embody the untamed spirit of the Last Frontier. It's in the melding of these locally sourced ingredients with international techniques that Anchorage's culinary alchemy truly shines. Picture savoring a plate of Alaska reindeer paired with a fragrant Thai curry, or indulging in an innovative sushi roll crafted from Alaska-caught fish.

The city's restaurants serve as epicenters of this culinary synergy, inviting diners to embark on a journey of flavors that transcend borders. Anchorage's historic streets, enriched by a mosaic of cultures, are adorned with eateries where tradition meets innovation. Step inside these establishments, and you'll find menus that narrate stories of exploration, trade, and the human desire to savor the world's diversity.

As you savor each bite, you're not merely tasting a dish—you're immersing yourself in Anchorage's ethos. It's a city that embraces the world while cherishing its own heritage, where the conversation between ingredients and techniques unfolds like a mesmerizing tale. Anchorage's culinary scene is an embodiment of the city's global spirit—a place where international flavors and local ingredients coalesce, leaving an indelible mark on both palate and memory.

So, prepare to embark on a journey through Anchorage's culinary tapestry, where every forkful is a step into a world of flavors that stretch beyond horizons. With each bite, you're not just enjoying a meal; you're partaking in the story of a city that honors the traditions of distant lands and the treasures of its own backyard. Welcome to Anchorage—a city that invites you to explore its diverse palates, where every dish tells a tale of unity through the universal language of food.

Where to Find the Best Food Trucks and Eateries

In the northern embrace of Anchorage, a gastronomic journey awaits—a journey that transcends traditional dining norms and immerses you in the vibrant tapestry of flavors found within its food trucks and eateries. Anchorage's culinary landscape is a harmonious blend of innovation, tradition, and global influences, a testament to a city that takes its culinary artistry seriously. Embark on a voyage of taste and discovery as we unveil the hidden gems that define Anchorage's best food trucks and eateries, a chapter in this city's epicurean narrative.

Street Food Fusion: Anchorage's Food Truck Culture

Anchorage's food truck culture is a thriving testament to the city's culinary prowess. Along bustling streets and at local events, these mobile kitchens dish out a tantalizing array of international cuisines, reinventing street food with creativity and flair. Venture to the Dimond Mall Food Truck Court, a gastronomic oasis that brings together an eclectic selection of vendors, each offering a unique journey into world flavors. Here, Thai curries dance with Mexican street tacos, and the aromatic embrace of Indian spices mingles with the boldness of American barbecue.

A Taste of Tradition: Indigenous Eateries

Delving deeper into Anchorage's culinary mosaic, one encounters eateries that pay homage to Alaska's rich indigenous heritage. These establishments seamlessly weave tradition with modern interpretations, curating menus that celebrate local ingredients and ancestral culinary techniques. At Arctic Roadrunner, the iconic reindeer hot dog stands as a symbol of Alaska's wilderness fare. And at cafes like Alaska Native Heritage Center Café, the flavors of the land are celebrated, showcasing dishes that have sustained communities for generations.

Harboring Seafood Splendor: Coastal Delights

Anchorage's proximity to the cold Alaskan waters gifts it with a bountiful array of seafood offerings that grace the menus of its eateries. Venture to Simon & Seaforts, where panoramic views of the Cook Inlet accompany succulent Alaskan king crab legs and perfectly seared halibut. The Bridge Seafood Restaurant offers a maritime ambiance as intricate as its culinary creations, where oysters on the half shell and smoked salmon share the spotlight with breathtaking views of the water.

Global Fare, Anchorage Flair: International Cuisine

Anchorage's international dining scene offers a passport to culinary traditions from around the world, each plate narrating a story of cultural fusion. Savor the complexity of flavors at Sourdough Mining Company, where steakhouse classics meet Alaskan inspiration. For a taste of Korea, embark on a culinary journey to Kumagoro, where authentic bibimbap and savory bulgogi transport you to the streets of Seoul.

Eateries with a View: Culinary Elevation

Eateries with scenic vistas elevate dining in Anchorage to an unmatched level of sensory experience. The Double Musky Inn enchants with its rustic elegance, serving up Cajun and Creole classics that transport you to the heart of Louisiana. As you savor each bite, take in the sprawling views of the Chugach Mountains—a sight that complements the culinary artistry.

Sweets and Treats: Indulgence Defined

No culinary exploration is complete without a sweet denouement, and Anchorage's dessert scene doesn't disappoint. Swing by Fire Island Rustic Bakeshop, where flaky croissants and artisanal pastries are crafted with meticulous attention to detail. For an ice cream experience unlike any other, indulge in unique flavors at Wild Scoops, where Alaskan ingredients shine in scoops of spruce tip and rhubarb sorbet.

In the realm of Anchorage's food trucks and eateries, culinary artistry thrives, offering a spectrum of flavors that beckon to the curious palate. From the vibrant diversity of street food to the nuanced interpretations of indigenous cuisine, each bite is a brushstroke on Anchorage's gastronomic canvas. Embark on this culinary odyssey, where you'll not only satisfy your appetite but also gain a deeper understanding of the cultural tapestry that defines this enchanting Alaskan city.

Anchorage after Dark

Nightlife Highlights: Bars, Breweries, and Lounges

When the sun dips below the Alaskan horizon, Anchorage transforms into a realm of captivating allure, where the city's nocturnal heartbeat resonates through its vibrant bars, breweries, and lounges. Anchorage's nightlife is not merely an afterthought—it's a harmonious ensemble that melds entertainment, craftsmanship, and a sense of camaraderie into an experience that captivates both locals and visitors alike. As the moon casts its gentle glow, allow yourself to be immersed in Anchorage's after-dark symphony—a symphony that crescendos with every sip, every laugh, and every connection forged.

Bars that Paint the Night with Delight:

Anchorage's bar scene is a canvas of diversity, where each venue tells its own story through its ambiance, libations, and patrons. From the historic charm of Glacier Brewhouse to the modern elegance of 49th State Brewing Co., the options are as varied as the Alaskan landscapes. Sip on handcrafted cocktails at Cabin Tavern, where mixology becomes an art form, or experience the timeless comfort of a neighborhood pub at Peanut Farm. Whether you seek a refined atmosphere or a casual gathering spot, Anchorage's bars invite you to unwind and engage in spirited conversations that flow like the spirits they serve.

Breweries: A Crafted Odyssey into Flavor:

For connoisseurs of finely crafted brews, Anchorage's breweries are an expedition into the world of hops, malts, and innovation. Midnight Sun Brewing Co., with its pioneering spirit, has been a beacon for beer enthusiasts, offering a spectrum of ales that reflect Alaska's rugged character. Anchorage Brewing Company, renowned for its avant-garde creations, tantalizes palates with barrel-aged wonders that defy convention. As the golden elixirs flow, embrace the camaraderie that's woven into the very essence of craft brewing—an invitation to revel in the intricate nuances of flavor and the shared joy of discovery.

Lounges: Where Elegance Meets Revelry:

Anchorage's lounges provide an intimate and sophisticated space for those seeking an evening of refined revelry. Slip into the opulent world of SubZero Lounge, where mixologists craft liquid artistry amidst an ambiance of understated luxury. If you crave a touch of nostalgia, Darwin's Theory takes you back in time with its speakeasy charm, offering expertly curated cocktails that pay homage to the classics. Anchorage's lounges transcend the ordinary, inviting you to indulge in the art of unwinding in settings where every detail is a testament to the pursuit of excellence.

The Nocturnal Melody: Live Music and Entertainment:

Anchorage's nightlife extends beyond libations; it's a stage for live music and entertainment that leaves an indelible mark on the senses. The Hard Rock Cafe Anchorage resonates with live performances that elevate your experience to a crescendo of rhythm and energy. For those seeking an evening of laughter, Koot's Comedy Club offers stand-up comedy that echoes through the night, leaving echoes of joy in its wake. Anchorage's nightlife isn't just about what you taste—it's about what you feel, what you hear, and the memories you create.

As the curtain falls on Anchorage's night, the vibrant tapestry of bars, breweries, and lounges remains etched in your memory—a symphony of taste, culture, and camaraderie that punctuates your journey. Anchorage's nocturnal allure isn't just about indulgence; it's about becoming part of a narrative—a narrative where each venue becomes a chapter, each drink an anecdote, and each encounter a shared experience that lingers long after the night has waned. Embrace Anchorage's after-dark charms, and allow its nightlife to serenade you into a world where the night is as rich and vivid as the day.

Live Music and Performance Venues
In the resounding heart of Anchorage, a symphony of cultural melodies comes to life as live music and

performance venues flourish. Anchorage's thriving arts scene is a testament to the city's commitment to artistic expression and community engagement. From intimate jazz ensembles to riveting theater productions, the city's live music and performance venues offer a captivating showcase of talent and creativity, underscoring Anchorage's status as a cultural hub in the heart of Alaska.

Anchorage Symphony Orchestra: The Epitome of Elegance

At the apex of Anchorage's musical prowess stands the Anchorage Symphony Orchestra—a beacon of classical refinement and artistic mastery. The grandeur of the Atwood Concert Hall, nestled within the Alaska Center for the Performing Arts, provides an exquisite backdrop for captivating symphonies and timeless compositions. Under the baton of accomplished conductors, the orchestra unfurls a rich tapestry of harmonies, enchanting audiences with performances that transcend time and culture.

Bear's Tooth Theatrepub: Fusion of Film and Music

For those seeking an amalgamation of artistic delights, the Bear's Tooth Theatrepub offers a unique fusion of film and live music. Anchorage's first theatrepub boasts a distinctive atmosphere where indie films flicker on screens as local musicians grace the stage. With its inviting ambience and delectable cuisine, this venue effortlessly weaves cinematic stories with live musical experiences, providing an unconventional yet immersive artistic encounter.

The Alaska Center for the Performing Arts: A Storied Stage

The Alaska Center for the Performing Arts stands as the epicenter of Anchorage's cultural vibrancy—a multidimensional nexus where world-class performances converge. From Broadway productions to contemporary dance, this venue's stages resonate with a diverse spectrum of artistic expressions. As the lights dim and the curtains rise, audiences are transported into realms of storytelling, innovation, and the boundless power of the performing arts.

Koot's - Anchorage's Legendary Pulse

Embracing the spirit of a true music sanctuary, Koot's offers an electrifying experience for those drawn to Anchorage's live music scene. A legendary institution, Koot's pulsates with the energy of local bands, cover artists, and genre-defying performances. The ambiance of Koot's is an embodiment of the city's vivacity—where laughter, camaraderie, and the strains of music meld into an unforgettable evening.

Williwaw Social: Where Eclecticism Thrives

In the heart of Anchorage's downtown, the Williwaw Social stands as a testament to the city's eclectic tastes. This multifaceted venue seamlessly transitions from an art gallery to a live music haven, featuring an array of performances that span genres and cultures. Williwaw Social is a reflection of Anchorage's open-minded embrace of artistic diversity, where innovation is celebrated and creative boundaries are pushed.

Community Enclaves and Emerging Stages

Beyond the established venues, Anchorage's live music and performance landscape thrives within local enclaves and emerging stages. From cozy cafes hosting acoustic serenades to open mics that give emerging artists a platform, these intimate settings embody the grassroots spirit of Anchorage's artistic tapestry. The magic of discovering a hidden gem of a performance space, where passion takes center stage, is a cherished experience that resonates deeply.

As you traverse Anchorage's live music and performance venues, you'll find yourself immersed in a cultural symphony that harmonizes tradition with innovation. Whether it's the refined strains of an orchestra, the pulsating rhythms of a downtown club, or the intimate melodies of a neighborhood cafe, Anchorage's musical landscape is a celebration of human expression—an echo of the city's collective soul. Prepare to be captivated, moved, and transported as Anchorage's stages come alive with the power of artistic resonance.

Aurora Borealis Watching

In the tranquil embrace of Anchorage, Alaska, nature unveils one of its most awe-inspiring and ethereal performances—the enchanting dance of the Aurora Borealis. As the curtain of night falls over the Alaskan skies, a celestial symphony of colors and light unfolds, captivating all who gather to witness this mesmerizing spectacle. Anchorage, known for its privileged position under the Auroral Oval, offers an unparalleled vantage point to partake in the mystical ballet of the Northern Lights, a celestial masterpiece that transcends the boundaries of imagination.

Spectacular Symphony of Light:

Aurora Borealis, the luminous phenomenon caused by solar particles colliding with Earth's atmosphere, transforms the night sky into a canvas of vivid hues. Anchorage's optimal position within the Auroral Oval—a region encircling the North Pole where the Northern Lights are frequently visible—grants visitors an exceptional chance to witness this ethereal display of light and color. As the charged particles interact with the gases in the atmosphere, they release radiant bands of green, pink, purple, and even red, creating an otherworldly spectacle that has entranced generations.

Ideal Conditions for Observation:

Anchorage's clear, unpolluted skies coupled with its relatively low light pollution make it an ideal destination for Aurora Borealis enthusiasts. While the lights may grace the sky on various nights, winter months, particularly from September to April, offer the most favorable conditions for observation. During these months, the extended darkness amplifies the radiance of the Northern Lights, creating a celestial panorama that remains etched in memory.

Strategic Locations for Viewing:

Venturing just beyond the city lights enhances the chances of an unobstructed view of the Aurora Borealis. Chugach State Park and nearby Eklutna Lake are favored locales, providing elevated viewpoints and pristine landscapes that complement the celestial show. For those who wish to remain closer to the city, Earthquake Park offers convenient accessibility and a unique urban perspective of the lights dancing over the Alaskan horizon.

The Dance of Preparation:

For travelers seeking to embrace this celestial marvel, preparation is key. Monitoring local aurora forecasts, which predict the likelihood and intensity of the Northern Lights, ensures optimal viewing conditions. Timing is crucial, as the lights are most active in the late evening and early morning hours. Warm clothing and patience become steadfast companions, as waiting for the Aurora Borealis to make its grand appearance is an experience that rewards both the heart and the senses.

A Journey of Ethereal Moments:

The experience of witnessing the Aurora Borealis in Anchorage transcends the realm of ordinary travel. Underneath the twinkling stars, as the lights weave their luminescent tapestry across the sky, visitors become part of an ancient and universal narrative—an enchanting story that unfolds with every ripple of color. It's a journey not just through time and space, but a journey within oneself—a moment of introspection and connection with the celestial wonders that have captivated humanity for millennia.

Conclusion:

In the quiet expanses of Anchorage, the Aurora Borealis graces the night sky with its ineffable beauty—a celestial ballet that ignites the imagination and touches the soul. Anchorage's strategic positioning, clear skies, and resplendent natural landscapes provide the stage for this ethereal performance. For those who seek to bask in the radiance of the Northern Lights, Anchorage offers an unparalleled opportunity to witness a celestial masterpiece—an experience that rekindles a sense of wonder and leaves an indelible mark on the heart.

Shopping in Anchorage

Souvenirs and Keepsakes

In the heart of Anchorage, a city that resonates with the majestic beauty of Alaska's wilderness and the vibrant pulse of urban life, lies a world of treasures waiting to be discovered. Anchorage's array of souvenirs and keepsakes are not merely trinkets; they encapsulate the essence of this captivating destination, allowing visitors to carry a piece of its unique charm home with them.

Artisan Crafts and Indigenous Art:

Anchorage's creative spirit finds expression in its local artisans and indigenous communities. Immerse yourself in the city's art galleries and boutiques, where you'll find handcrafted jewelry, intricate wood carvings, and exquisite beadwork. Each piece carries the stories of its makers, celebrating their cultural heritage and artistic prowess.

Alaskan Keepsake Jewelry:

From delicate silver necklaces adorned with whale tails to stunning earrings shaped like snowflakes, Anchorage's jewelry shops offer a plethora of keepsakes inspired by the region's wildlife and natural wonders. These finely crafted pieces capture the essence of Alaska's untamed landscapes and make for cherished mementos.

Local Flavors:

Anchorage's culinary scene is a treasure trove of flavors that beckon to be taken home. Indulge in jars of wild berry preserves, smoked salmon, and gourmet chocolates crafted with Alaskan ingredients. These delectable treats offer a taste of Anchorage's gastronomic excellence long after your journey ends.

Outdoor Gear and Adventure Essentials:

For those drawn to Anchorage's rugged landscapes and thrilling outdoor activities, local shops offer an array of high-quality outdoor gear. From sturdy backpacks to versatile clothing designed to withstand Alaska's elements, these items are both practical and symbolic of your adventurous spirit.

Native Arts and Crafts Markets:

Visiting Anchorage's native arts and crafts markets is an immersive cultural experience. Explore bustling marketplaces where you can interact with local artisans, admire traditional handicrafts, and acquire items like woven baskets, intricate masks, and storytelling totems.

Local Artwork and Photography:

Anchorage's natural beauty has long been an inspiration for artists and photographers. Galleries throughout the city showcase stunning landscapes, capturing the interplay of light and shadows against the backdrop of mountains and waterways. These artworks allow you to bring Anchorage's breathtaking vistas into your home.

Books and Literature:

Anchorage's literary scene offers a rich selection of books, ranging from tales of exploration and adventure to insightful guides on Alaska's flora, fauna, and native cultures. These volumes provide a deeper understanding of the region's history and natural wonders.

Ethical and Sustainable Products:

Anchorage's commitment to sustainability extends to its offerings of eco-friendly souvenirs. From recycled materials transformed into innovative art pieces to ethically sourced clothing and accessories, these choices reflect the city's dedication to responsible consumption.

In Anchorage, the act of choosing a souvenir becomes a journey of discovering the city's heart and soul. Each item embodies the spirit of Alaska's wilderness and the warmth of its people. As you peruse the city's markets, galleries, and boutiques, you'll find that the treasures you bring home are not just material possessions but gateways to cherished memories and connections that endure long after your visit. Anchorage's souvenirs and keepsakes transcend the ordinary, becoming tangible reminders of the extraordinary experiences that define your time in this remarkable destination.

Native Arts and Crafts

In the heart of Anchorage, a city adorned with natural wonders, a vibrant tapestry of culture awaits those who seek to delve into the rich heritage of Alaska's Native communities. Anchorage isn't merely a destination; it's a gateway to a world where tradition, craftsmanship, and artistic expression converge. The realm of Native arts and crafts beckons, inviting travelers to embark on a journey that transcends time, where the past and present intertwine to create captivating stories of indigenous creativity.

Unveiling Tradition: A Glimpse into Alaska's Indigenous Heritage

The soul of Anchorage's Native arts and crafts lies in the tapestry of indigenous heritage. As you traverse the city's cultural landscape, you'll encounter galleries, museums, and artisan workshops that serve as gateways to the traditions of Alaska's Native peoples. Anchorage's commitment to preserving these traditions is evident in institutions such as the Anchorage Museum, where meticulously curated exhibits offer insight into the artistic evolution of Alaska's indigenous communities.

Crafting History: A Journey through Artistic Expression

Every artifact, every piece of art, carries a story—a narrative woven by the hands of those who have shaped and passed down these traditions through generations. Anchorage provides a platform to witness this living history firsthand. Handcrafted jewelry, intricate beadwork, masterful wood carvings, and detailed textiles stand as a testament to the cultural significance embedded in every stroke and stitch. The native galleries and cultural centers that grace the city's thoroughfares offer a window into the artistic expressions that have defined Alaska's Native communities.

Artisanal Encounters: Connecting with the Creators

Anchorage's cultural journey transcends the confines of a gallery. Engaging with the artisans behind these masterpieces is an invitation to understand the stories, techniques, and inspirations that breathe life into their creations. Art walks and indigenous craft fairs provide a platform to meet the artists, forging connections that resonate far beyond the transaction. Conversations become a bridge between cultures, enabling visitors to appreciate the significance of each crafted piece on a deeper level.

Cultural Immersion: Celebrating the Craftsmanship

Throughout the year, Anchorage's events calendar is adorned with celebrations that honor the vibrancy of Native arts and crafts. Festivals such as the

Alaska Native Heritage Month Celebration and the Alaska Federation of Natives Convention offer immersive experiences, where visitors can witness traditional dance performances, participate in hands-on workshops, and engage in conversations that illuminate the profound role of artistic expression in indigenous culture.

Supporting a Legacy: Owning a Piece of Tradition

Anchorage's journey into the world of Native arts and crafts goes beyond observation—it offers the opportunity to own a piece of this rich heritage. Handcrafted souvenirs become more than mere keepsakes; they carry the essence of Alaska's Native culture, becoming cherished reminders of an immersive cultural exploration.

In Closing

Anchorage's Native arts and crafts scene is an exploration of authenticity, an odyssey through the creative pulse of indigenous heritage. As you navigate this cultural landscape, you're invited not only to appreciate the artistic expressions of Alaska's Native peoples but also to engage in a dialogue that transcends cultural boundaries. Anchorage isn't just a destination; it's an immersive encounter with tradition, a symphony of creative expression that resonates with the heart and soul of those who seek to uncover the cultural treasures within.

Retail Therapy: Malls and Boutiques

In Anchorage, Alaska's urban gem nestled amidst untamed wilderness, the pursuit of retail therapy transcends the ordinary. Anchorage's dynamic retail landscape is a testament to its unique character—a blend of rugged charm and cosmopolitan flair. From bustling malls that house international brands to eclectic boutiques that showcase local artistry, Anchorage's shopping scene offers a diverse and captivating experience that mirrors the city's multifaceted identity.

Malls:

Anchorage's malls stand as modern havens of shopping excellence, seamlessly merging urban convenience with the promise of Alaskan adventure just beyond their doors. Anchorage 5th Avenue Mall, an architectural marvel in the heart of downtown, embodies this fusion. Here, discerning shoppers can indulge in luxury fashion, jewelry, and cosmetics from renowned international brands, juxtaposed against the backdrop of snow-capped peaks that peer through the city's skyline. Anchorage 5th Avenue Mall isn't just a shopping destination—it's an immersive experience that bridges the gap between metropolitan sophistication and the Alaskan spirit.

Boutiques:

For those who seek a more personalized and artisanal shopping experience, Anchorage's boutiques beckon with an allure of their own. The city's vibrant arts and crafts community finds its voice in boutiques like Dos Manos, where locally crafted jewelry, ceramics, and textiles take center stage. Here, visitors can not only purchase meticulously crafted pieces but also engage with the creators themselves, enriching their understanding of Alaskan artistry.

If exploration of indigenous artistry is your calling, then the Alaska Native Arts Foundation Gallery is a haven of authenticity. This gallery, dedicated to promoting indigenous artists, showcases an array of traditional and contemporary works, from intricate wood carvings to masterfully woven baskets. Each piece carries within it a story that resonates with the ancestral spirits of Alaska, offering visitors an opportunity to take home a piece of Alaskan heritage.

Flea Markets:

Anchorage's retail scene extends beyond conventional malls and boutiques, embracing the spontaneity and camaraderie of flea markets. The Anchorage Market and Festival, a vibrant celebration of local culture, arts, and crafts, transforms downtown streets into an open-air market where treasures from across the state converge. From handcrafted jewelry and apparel to locally sourced food products, the market is a sensory delight that resonates with the pulse of the city.

The Alaskan Souvenir:

No exploration of Anchorage's retail offerings would be complete without a nod to the quintessential Alaskan souvenir—the iconic ulu knife. Woven deeply into indigenous culture, the ulu knife is a symbol of utility and craftsmanship. It finds its home in boutiques and markets across the city, and acquiring one not only offers a functional keepsake but also connects travelers to the age-old traditions of Alaska's native peoples.

In the realm of retail therapy, Anchorage unfolds as a vibrant canvas that reflects the diverse tapestry of its inhabitants and its unique geographical setting. The juxtaposition of luxurious malls against a backdrop of wilderness, the interplay of boutique artistry and indigenous heritage, and the communal spirit of open-air markets come together to create an unparalleled shopping experience. Anchorage invites you to embrace the city's retail haven—a journey that transcends mere shopping and offers an insight into the very soul of this captivating Alaskan urban oasis.

Anchorage on a Budget

Affordable Accommodation Options

In the heart of Alaska's vibrant urban landscape lies Anchorage—a city that marries natural grandeur with cultural charm. As you embark on your journey to this captivating destination, the question of accommodation invariably arises. Fear not, for Anchorage extends a welcoming embrace to travelers seeking comfort without compromising on quality. From the rugged Alaskan wilderness to the city's thriving center, a range of affordable accommodation options beckon, ensuring your stay is marked by both elegance and budget-friendly practicality.

Boutique Inns and Guesthouses: Anchorage boasts a delightful array of boutique inns and guesthouses that promise an intimate and cozy stay. These accommodations are often tucked within charming neighborhoods, offering a sense of local immersion. With a focus on personalized service and distinctive decor, these hidden gems provide an affordable escape that evokes the spirit of the city.

Modern Motels and Lodges: Anchorage's modern motels and lodges present an attractive blend of convenience and comfort. Located both within the city limits and its outskirts, these establishments provide a comfortable retreat for the budget-conscious traveler. Expect well-appointed rooms, essential amenities, and a range of accommodation sizes to suit your needs.

Extended Stay Hotels: For those looking to immerse themselves in Anchorage's vibrant culture for an extended period, the city offers a selection of extended stay hotels. These accommodations are tailored to provide a homely environment, often featuring kitchenettes or full kitchens. With competitive rates for extended stays, they allow you to explore Anchorage at your own pace without exceeding your budget.

Hostels and Budget Inns: Anchorage's array of hostels and budget inns epitomizes affordability without compromising on comfort. Ideal for solo travelers or those seeking to connect with fellow explorers, these accommodations offer shared dormitories or private rooms. Modern amenities and communal spaces create a convivial atmosphere, fostering interactions and shared experiences.

Vacation Rentals: Anchorage's vacation rental market provides an avenue for travelers to enjoy the comforts of home away from home. From cozy apartments to spacious homes, these rentals are particularly appealing for families or groups seeking affordable lodging. The added advantage of kitchen facilities allows you to create your own culinary experiences while staying on budget.

Campgrounds and RV Parks: For the adventurous souls who revel in nature's embrace, Anchorage's campgrounds and RV parks offer an authentic Alaskan experience. Set against breathtaking backdrops, these options cater to both tent campers and RV enthusiasts. With affordable rates and proximity to outdoor adventures, they beckon to those seeking an affordable yet immersive stay.

As you traverse Anchorage's diverse landscapes, you'll discover that affordable accommodation options abound. Whether you're seeking the charm of a boutique inn, the modern amenities of a motel, or the camaraderie of a hostel, Anchorage extends an open invitation to explore its offerings. Here, comfort and affordability intertwine seamlessly, ensuring that your journey through Alaska's urban gem is marked by restful nights and budget-friendly elegance.

Low-Cost Dining and Activities

In the captivating embrace of Anchorage, where the natural wonders of Alaska converge with vibrant urban life, lies an opportunity to experience the city's charm without breaking the bank. Anchorage, often perceived as a destination for the adventurous and well-heeled, unveils a lesser-known facet—low-cost dining and activities that allow budget-conscious travelers to savor the city's essence without compromise. Embrace a journey where affordability meets authenticity, and discover how

Anchorage can be explored on a budget while still relishing every moment.

Culinary Adventures That Won't Break the Bank:

In a city renowned for its culinary scene, savoring delectable fare need not be a costly endeavor. Anchorage's food trucks are hidden gems, offering a treasure trove of flavors at wallet-friendly prices. Feast on gourmet sandwiches, mouthwatering tacos, and globally inspired dishes that reflect the city's cultural diversity. Immerse yourself in the energetic atmosphere of Anchorage's farmers' markets, where fresh produce, artisanal cheeses, and local delicacies await your discerning palate. These markets aren't just about shopping; they're a vibrant feast for the senses and a budget-friendly way to connect with the local food culture.

Thrifty Explorations That Inspire:

Anchorage's captivating landscapes and cultural treasures can be enjoyed without straining your budget. Immerse yourself in the city's outdoor splendor with a leisurely stroll or bike ride along the Tony Knowles Coastal Trail. This scenic pathway offers breathtaking waterfront views and opportunities for wildlife spotting, all without incurring any costs. Nature enthusiasts will find solace in the serene ambiance of Anchorage's parks, such as Town Square Park, providing a tranquil retreat for picnics and people-watching.

Cultural Insights without the Price Tag:

Anchorage's cultural tapestry is rich and diverse, and you can delve into its intricacies without worrying about your wallet. The Anchorage Museum, a treasure trove of Alaskan art and history, offers free admission on select days and is an ideal spot to immerse yourself in the city's heritage. Don't miss the opportunity to explore local art galleries and studios, where creativity flourishes and entry is often complimentary.

Bargains and Beyond:

Uncover hidden gems in Anchorage's shopping scene that cater to budget-conscious travelers. Seek out thrift stores and consignment shops that offer unique finds at pocket-friendly prices. These establishments often reveal a tapestry of vintage clothing, antique collectibles, and eclectic items that make for memorable souvenirs without straining your budget.

Navigating the City on a Dime:

Public transportation in Anchorage offers an affordable means of getting around the city. The People Mover buses are not only budget-friendly but also provide an opportunity to engage with the local rhythm of life. Utilize these services to access attractions, neighborhoods, and dining spots with ease, all while keeping costs in check.

In conclusion, Anchorage's allure is not confined to the well-heeled traveler. Embrace the city's low-cost dining options and engage in budget-friendly activities that capture the spirit of the Alaskan experience. Anchorage on a budget is an invitation to explore, connect, and savor the essence of the city without compromising on authenticity. Let Anchorage be your canvas for adventure, a place where affordability and exploration harmoniously intersect, and where the treasures of the city are accessible to all who seek them.

Free and Low-Cost Attractions

In the heart of Anchorage, Alaska's urban jewel, a wealth of experiences awaits discerning travelers, each unveiling a tapestry of cultural, natural, and historical treasures. Amidst the majestic landscapes and vibrant urban pulse, the city offers a bounty of free and low-cost attractions, a testament to its commitment to welcoming visitors with open arms. Delve into a realm where value meets enrichment, and exploration need not come at a high price.

Anchorage Museum at Rasmuson Center: An artistic and historical haven, the Anchorage Museum beckons with its impressive collection that chronicles Alaska's diverse heritage. While entry might require a modest fee, the museum often offers special days where admission is waived, providing an opportunity to immerse oneself in Alaskan culture, art, and history.

Tony Knowles Coastal Trail: Nature enthusiasts and avid photographers will find solace along the captivating Tony Knowles Coastal Trail. With breathtaking vistas of the surrounding mountains and the shimmering waters of Cook Inlet, this trail offers a scenic escape where the wonders of Alaska's wilderness are on full display.

Ship Creek Viewing Platform: For an authentic Alaskan experience, venture to the Ship Creek Viewing Platform. This vantage point allows visitors to witness local anglers casting their lines in hopes of reeling in prized salmon—a snapshot of Anchorage's fishing heritage against the backdrop of the city's skyline.

Earthquake Park: Delve into Anchorage's history at Earthquake Park, a poignant tribute to the 1964 Great Alaska Earthquake. Amidst scenic trails, visitors can explore interpretive exhibits that provide insights into the powerful forces of nature and their impact on the landscape.

Alaska Veterans Memorial: Paying homage to the brave souls who have served the nation, the Alaska Veterans Memorial stands as a testament to honor and remembrance. The tranquil setting invites contemplation and gratitude, while the names inscribed on the memorial serve as a reminder of sacrifices made.

Saturday Market and Sunday Market: Experience the vibrant energy of Anchorage's local artisans, musicians, and food vendors at the Saturday Market and Sunday Market. These open-air markets showcase Alaska's creativity, offering a platform for unique crafts, delectable treats, and live entertainment.

Delaney Park Strip: Known as the "People's Park," Delaney Park Strip is a serene urban oasis that hosts events, festivals, and gatherings throughout the year. It's a place where locals and visitors converge to partake in recreational activities, cultural celebrations, and the simple pleasure of relaxation.

Cultural Performances at Town Square: Anchorage's Town Square transforms into a hub of cultural enrichment during the summer months. With free outdoor performances ranging from live music to dance presentations, the square becomes a stage where diverse art forms come to life.

Local Libraries: Anchorage's public libraries offer more than just books—they provide gateways to knowledge and community engagement. Many libraries host free events, workshops, and lectures that invite visitors to expand their horizons and connect with fellow explorers.

Scenic Drives: Sometimes, the allure of Anchorage lies in the journey itself. Embark on a scenic drive along the Seward Highway or the Glenn Highway, where awe-inspiring landscapes unfold at every turn. These routes provide an opportunity to witness the grandeur of Alaska's wilderness without requiring an entry fee.

As you traverse Anchorage's free and low-cost attractions, you'll discover that the city's true riches lie not only in its awe-inspiring landscapes and cultural offerings but also in its commitment to making its treasures accessible to all. Anchorage stands as a testament to the notion that exploration need not be confined to lavish expenditures; rather, it is the spirit of discovery and appreciation that defines the true value of a journey.

Conclusion

As the final chapter of "Anchorage Unveiled: Your Essential Companion to Embracing the Wonders of Alaska's Gateway City" draws to a close, we find ourselves at the end of a remarkable journey—a journey that has transcended pages and maps, guiding you through the heart and soul of a city that leaves an indelible mark on all who venture within its embrace.

From the sprawling landscapes that greet your senses to the intricate tapestry of neighborhoods painted with the strokes of creativity, Anchorage has revealed itself as a city of boundless allure. It has whispered stories of resilience, unity, and a profound connection with nature that enriches both body and spirit.

With each page turned, you've explored the seasons that dance through Anchorage's skies, offering a kaleidoscope of experiences that transform the city's streets and trails into stages of wonder. From winter's snowy wonderland to summer's midnight sun, Anchorage has unveiled itself as a city that thrives in all its seasons, inviting you to be part of its vibrant narrative.

As you embarked on your journey through the chapters dedicated to downtown's urban heartbeat, practical tips for travelers, and the enchanting districts that weave Anchorage's narrative, you've come to understand that this city isn't just a place—

it's an invitation. An invitation to partake in the celebration of culture, to savor the bounty of the earth's offerings, and to immerse yourself in a community that thrives on inclusivity and shared experiences.

And now, as we bid adieu to the pages of "Anchorage Unveiled," may you carry with you the essence of this gateway city—an essence that blends the urban pulse with the wilderness' serenity, that unites creativity and authenticity, and that fosters connections both with fellow travelers and the very heart of the city itself.

In your future explorations, may the lessons learned within these pages guide you, not only through Anchorage's captivating streets but through the wider world as well. As you uncover new destinations, may you remember the warmth of Alaskan hospitality, the majesty of untamed landscapes, and the power of a city that embraces you as its own.

With Anchorage's lasting embrace etched into your memories, may your travels be forever enriched, your horizons expanded, and your heart open to the profound magic that awaits when we explore with open eyes, open hearts, and the spirit of adventure.

Farewell, dear traveler, and may your journey be forever intertwined with the treasures Anchorage has so generously unveiled.

Made in the USA
Middletown, DE
22 January 2024

48333716R00096